sp**O**rts **O**utreach

Steve Connor has made another invaluable contribution to the 'Great Commission' by providing his second book *Sports Outreach* as a practical resource for the sporting world. His expertise in the field of sports ministry is unparalleled when it comes to a global perspective. Having run successful sports ministries in both the UK as well as the USA, gives Steve a voice that should be listened to by any who desire to minister through sport. This is a complete resource as it combines Biblical principles and practical applications for all levels and associations who have are interested in sharing the gospel through sport.

Dr Terry Franson, Dean of Students, Azusa Pacific University

Steve Connor has recognized that the local church is the key denominator in the spiritual growth of any athlete. He has a particular heart for young people with a passion for sport and lays out a clear game plan for reaching this age group with the life changing message of Christ. This book will spur on those who wish to bring heaven down onto the games fields of this world.

Bryan Mason, UK Coordinator
Church Sports & Recreation Ministry (Christians in Sport)

Sports Outreach provides the essentials to craft a quality sports ministry that is biblically sound. Steve Connor, more than most others in sports ministry, has carefully extracted biblical principles and successfully put these principles and supporting methods into practice. This biblically-focused manual of sports ministry is based on solid principles with extensive examples and easy-to-apply models and is delivered in the language of the sportsperson. The aspiring sports outreach leader as well as the seasoned sports minister will both have much to gain from Steve Connor's insights and methods of sports ministry. *Sports Outreach* is currently the most comprehensive manual to follow as a guide to doing effective sports ministry.'

Dr Bud Williams, Wheaton College

In a world that is dominated by sport, music and fashion Steve Connor has given an invaluable tool to the church at large. He shares well thought out reasons why Christians need to engage with the world of sport. He has managed to create a manual that will be valuable to all who have a passion to communicate the gospel, regardless of their sporting credentials. He writes in such a manner that allows the discerning reader to make the necessary adjustments to transfer his sports models of ministry into other activity-based ministries. This is a book that is full of practical advice and sound wisdom It is a how to book that is not afraid to answer the question why?

Rev Albert Bogle, Evangelist and Parish Minister in the Church of Scotland

Since Steve started his sports ministry thousands of young men and women have learnt what it means to know Christ and to grow to maturity in following him in the sports community. Indeed, we are now seeing those who started at camp as teenagers in leadership positions themselves, taking responsibility for sharing the gospel and nurturing faith amongst young sportspeople. Christians In Sport thank God for Steve Connor!

Graham Daniels, Director of Christians in Sport

sports Outreach

principles + practice for successful sports ministry

steve connor

CHRISTIAN FOCUS PUBLICATIONS

ISBN 1-85792-724-9

© Copyright Steve Connor 2003

Published in 2003
by
Christian Focus Publications, Ltd.
Geanies House, Fearn, Tain,
Ross-shire, IV20 1TW, Scotland

www.christianfocus.com

Printed and bound in Scotland by
Bell & Bain Ltd., Glasgow

Design by Alister MacInnes
Typeset in BakerSignet and AgencyFB

CONTENTS

Models of Sports Ministry: Objectives determine activities (Continued)

Acknowledgements

Thank you so much to my wife Michelle who will stop on a dime and listen to every idea I have – both the goofy and good. To Anne Norrie, my editor, who can unravel confusion with poise and joy. I am grateful for Coach Rex for leading me to Christ, and Fellowship of Christian Athletes for their faithful commitment to present Christ to athletes and coaches and all whom they influence over all the years. For Jack Vandiver and Athletes in Action for their faithful commitment to discipleship and spiritual maturity. For Christians in Sport for their dogged determination to do sports ministry in adherence to Scripture: 'correctly handling the word of truth'. To Eddie Waxer and Roger Oswald for teaching sports ministry to us all around the world. And lastly for Professor Jerry Root whose encouragement and counsel are on every page.

**Special thanks to Cully – your illustrations speak
almost as loud as your servant heart.**

Dedication

To Harry
My awesome son
and faithful prayer warrior

This book is for all those who have been thrown into swimming pools, jammed their cars full of supplies and kids, sacrificed hobbies, hunted down speakers, lost countless hours of sleep with hurting parents, given away their best tennis racquets, allowed their carpets to be wrecked, purchased hundreds of Mars Bars, disciplined the goofy, loved the unloved, been asked to do it all again next week, and have rarely been thanked.

For all those who yearn for vibrant and not so vibrant sporty people to give their hearts, lives and sport fully to our Saviour Jesus Christ – this book is for those with a heart for ministry.

INTRODUCTION
THE BIG PICTURE

LET me ask you a question: if a musician, let's say a piano player, walks into your church for the first time; would your minister or church leaders know how to best mobilise their skills and talents for the cause of Christ and the health of the church?

How about an athlete? If a sportsperson, let's say a football player, walks into your church for the first time; would your minister or church leaders know how to best mobilise <u>their</u> skills and talents for the cause of Christ and the health of the church?

The church historically knows how to involve musicians in the life of the church, which we applaud, but there is this massive group of people, sports people, that can not identify or feel alienated and marginalized by the church. This same group has a huge influence on how our culture is shaped. **So how is your church's Sports Ministry doing?**
Sports Outreach is a resource to the local church.

 A society looking up to athletes as heroes must find heroes looking up to God. **Wendel Deyo**

Sports ministry is developing around the world. Though certainly many ventures have been attempted with measured success and failure, there are very limited evangelistic resources and little thoughtful reflection in this important field. The objectives of this book are to encourage, explain and model sports ministry to ministers and lay leaders. Our goal is to have a resource that will train the church to effectively advance God's Kingdom in and through the world of sport. Sports ministry is merely a vehicle for someone who is in the world of sport (at varied levels) to tell another athlete about their greater love. We assume if you are reading this book our Lord has given you three great loves: a love for Him, a love for sports people and a love for sport. Those loves are no accident, it is a calling.

SPORTS OUTREACH

Big picture

Exercise your talent?

Our Lord has given us an eternity to live with Him but only a finite time to build His Kingdom on earth. He has given you unique gifts and abilities to make an impact, to respond to His goodness in obedience. You have been gifted and if you are looking at this book it is my hunch that you want to make that impact in the world of sport. God equips His people with special gifts to reach His people, to make a concerted effort to reach a distinctive group of people that are outside of Christ's faith community. Historically we see our Lord using faithful and obedient people for His purposes in reaching the lost. Our Lord is sufficient and by 'His mercy' (2 Cor. 4:1) will give His obedient children special ways to serve Him. We are given a limited amount of time and resources and we are to use these as effectively as possible. The world of sport is one of those strategic areas in the twenty-first century.

What is this?

This is a training manual and resource for developing sports ministry in your local church. Sports ministry is rapidly emerging as a vital component of the ongoing ministry of the local church as well as an effective tool for evangelism around the world. Unfortunately, very few resources are available. As I speak to Christians around the world an ongoing request is for a good practical supply of sporty biblical materials to reach, in particular, the youth and men of the church.

Why do you need it?

This book is in response to those churches that desperately want to impact their communities (to be salt and light) for Christ, specifically those in the environment of sport. The value of this book is to give biblical principles of ministry that will resource anyone interested in reaching the world of sport for Christ. Many Christian universities are exploring curricula for sports ministry. The Fellowship of Christian Athletes is now the biggest youth ministry in the US (arguably the biggest youth ministry in the world) with an estimated twenty thousand volunteers, but with few resources that help explain the whys and hows of ministry. Everywhere I go in the United Kingdom and throughout Europe I wish I had a book like this available.

What's in it?

- Biblical principles and strategy for sports ministry.
- Ingredients of a healthy sports ministry.
- Ideas to train and sustain leadership.
- Ideas on how to develop sports ministry.
- Healthy church models.
- Practical training tips for camps and missions, big events and small groups.
- Tools for equipping others to do sports ministry throughout the country.

Because of the nature of sport nothing dates quicker than sports ministry tracts and testimonies. So this book will attempt to focus on themes of enduring relevance, not on sports personalities or testimonies.

SPORTS OUTREACH

Who can use it?

I would want the serious athlete and concerned grandma alike to say, 'I can use this book – I can do sports ministry'.

Learn the language

Sports ministry is not the be-all and end-all of ministry – just one tool the master carpenter uses. When a missionary ventures off to another country and culture, language skills are vital. You can feel intimidated ministering to athletes if you are not inclined to sport. The barriers of foreign culture may seem less insurmountable than learning the nuances of a three-point stance, a forearm rip and swim technique (American Football jargon). But take heart, you don't need to be a superstar – having an elementary grasp of sport and ministry or finding someone that does will work. Are you willing to learn another language?

 After speaking evangelistically at a big event in England I was asked to follow up with a seminar on 'sports ministry'. It is always interesting to see who turns up. After years of doing these seminars I have met all types. Some people feel you have to be a great pro to be involved in sports ministry. If that were the case we would not have much of a movement. Some people want to do sports ministry because they will feel 'sporty' around sports people. They usually overcompensate their lack of talent by wearing all the right brands of sporting clothes, they don't play well, but they look good! These types do not last long because the novelty wears off fast and then they are faced with a lot of work. Some people have a wonderful but unarticulated calling in their lives to reach their sports world for Christ. They have this passion but are not sure if it really is a legitimate calling. These people are great, it is as if you are mining for gold and come up with a pure nugget. Others aren't sure of sports ministry and show up to check it out. These people are fun as you develop a foundation for theology and encourage them to use their unique gifts for God. Then there is the last group, the people that think that if it's fun it certainly can't be Christian ministry. They usually sit in the back with their arms folded a scowl on their face and waiting for you to say something they do not agree with.

At this particular seminar we waited for the room to fill up. I was not surprised at who sat where. Just before we started, an old granny walked in. I could see some of the boys rolling their eyes in the back of their heads, like what is she doing here? She was small and moving awfully slow. I have to admit that my first thought was, she must be in the wrong place, and is looking for the 'knitting for Jesus' seminar. She sat down right across from me so I asked, with a sheepish grin, so what's your sport? She laughed and got the humour fast. And I have never forgotten her reply. She said, 'Oh, dear I am not into sport, but my two grandsons will not go to church, they think it is for fuddy-duddies like me. But they are sports-mad! So I want to learn the language of sport and sports ministry so I can reach those two precious boys for Christ.' I did not teach her nearly anything as much as she taught me in that seminar. In Christ we have strange bedfellows and are called to proclaim Christ in some strange places. It is His ministry and our Lord who is, in some ways, unpredictable and will use anyone He chooses.

A broad range of people can be involved in sports ministry, from lay leaders and young people to youth pastors, ministers and Sunday school teachers. Any person who desires the church to be a bridge to his or her sporting community is eligible for sports ministry. The main principles highlighted are attainable by a varied audience. You don't have to be a professional athlete to use them! The book's function is twofold. The first two sections are training tools, and the third is more of a resource tool. Often my co-workers are made up of youth workers, teachers, coaches and athletic lay leader types, but some of the best I have had are dedicated mums and dads and even that special granny. They also have a varied experience and understanding of ministry. Obviously we rarely meet a young person that will make it to the professional ranks, but their zeal for sport is just as, if not more, intense. And the all-important 'spiritual aspect' is also tragically neglected. Sports ministry is purely an avenue for the gospel for those who may not be reached by Christ in any other way. This book is meant for the person keen to help their church have a Christian presence in the world of sport at the local level.

* I am writing for several different sports cultures. I don't care if you call your ministry Sports Outreach, Christians in Sport or Sports Ministry, our concern is reaching sports people for Christ and ministering with excellence. This book will go to over eight different countries. For clarification I have decided to use 'athelete' in the generic form, not merely track and field.

 The pages with this icon at the top are reproducible – I hope you will find them useful handouts for your team leaders or for your church partners in the ministry.

CHAPTER ONE
WHY IT WORKS

EFFICACY OF SPORTS MINISTRY

Sports Ministry is Old– but New

SINCE Jesus' resurrection the challenge of communicating our faith in Christ has historically been a fearsome pleasure. Generation after generation of obedient followers have pushed methodological confines to respond to Christ's Great Commission to: 'Go and make disciples.' Brave and aggressive followers of Christ have fought the resistance of other Christians who have opposed new ideas in evangelism. Change is threatening, Christians wanting to be obedient to their Creator can rightfully and wrongfully impede the transmission of the gospel. Ironically, sport is older than Christianity, yet today in many churches it may seem avant-garde. Obviously the Apostle Paul found sport a useful means to express God's truth through metaphor, *'Run in such a way as to get the prize' (1 Cor.9:24), 'For physical training is of some value, but godliness has value for all things' (1 Tim 4:8).* The body of Christ, God's church, seems to have a new awareness of sport and the value to communicate God's truth in sporting environments. More and more churches are having golf days, coaching clinics, sports services and leisure activities with evangelistic aims – ministering to people who the churches have previously shunned. This section gives evidence of the range, diversity, effectiveness and appeal of sports ministry. I hope it will also encourage and motivate workers to see the scope of experience from an historic perspective. Sport has the ability to build bridges in relationships and transcend cultural barriers in a world that is more and more compartmentalized. The vast majority of active participating sports people are young, but sports ministry can be a useful tool for anyone with a desire to reach the world of sport for Christ.

SPORTS OUTREACH

 ## Sport helps us reach 'Joe Average'

I was asked by an average church outside of Edinburgh to help them develop a cohesive strategy for reaching a certain community for Christ. The minister was adamant that their limited investment in evangelism over the past five years was not bringing in much fruit. 'It was not effective investment of our resources, we will be held accountable'. Much of their investment was trying to reach out to the fringe and disenfranchised (mainly kids in trouble and drug addicts), through a series of failed programmes. There is a direct mandate to minister to the poor and disenfranchised, I certainly did not want to dilute their efforts no matter how futile they seemed. The church leaders said they were still committed to reaching the 'fringe' but they realized they had drastically turned their backs on the majority – the 'Joe-average'. The minister said, 'Steve what does Joe-average like to do? He likes sport!'

The motivation, training and methodology of sports ministry were installed and the church over time saw direct fruit. Families were being reached, children were being reached and young adult males were finding their way to the church. Sport builds bridges into communities.

Postscript: Joe-average helps the disenfranchised.

The church in Edinburgh does not have a perfect sports ministry. They would say, 'far from it', but they are seeing fruit in unexpected places. Speaking to the minister two years after implementing the programme I was encouraged to hear that not only was 'Joe Average' being reached with the good news of Jesus Christ but an interesting by-product of sports ministry was occurring. The minister told me, 'We are mentoring Joe-average and you know what they want to do? Reach the lost! Go back into the schools and streets and minister, especially to those marginalized by society – those that we tried to get to in the first place.'

Sports Ministry Helps you 'Play-Away'!

Playing at home is easier than playing away! Home-field advantage is inspiring and more fun. The familiar dynamics of the dressing room as you prepare for the competition, the stadium filled with the accustomed and almost subconscious amalgamation of sights and sounds (popcorn and cigar smoke, team colours, familiar announcers, and cheering crowds) all rush your senses and give you confidence. To once again step onto the familiar surface of your home pitch (fields) is as affirming as wearing a well-fitting pair of old boots. There certainly is strategy in using your 'home pitch' for your advantage. I know of coaches who, on their home astro-turf, run plays towards the grain in the nap, knowing very well how slippery the old pitch is to the unaccustomed feet of an opponent. In Los Angeles it was always an advantage to compete 'at home' as your opponent was unaccustomed to playing in smog. Towards the end of the games the players that were not acclimatised to smog were always wheezing and gasping for air. It is no coincidence that British golfers win more British Opens because amidst the most miserable weather conditions they are fine! Playing at home is also so convenient, you don't have to fight buses, planes and trains.

On the flipside playing 'away' is harder. Wheaton College used to always tune up in the preseason American football by playing the inmates at Joliet prison (now closed, it was one of the most notorious prisons in America). It was daunting, you walked through the gates, you heard the prisoners yelling at the predominantly white middle-class Christian college students whose only experience of prison was what they had seen at the movies. Strange people, strange smells and a strange atmosphere all lend themselves to distraction and intimidation. The players for Joliet prison always got home-field advantage, they never played away!

> *We feel we are making a difference because we are so important to ourselves. We have created a phenomenal subculture with our own media, entertainment, educational system, and political hierarchy so we have the sense that we are doing a lot. But what we've really done is create a ghetto that is easily dismissed by the rest of society.* **Roaring Lambs**, Bob Briner

The church has been pretty good at playing at home for several centuries, but not so good at playing 'away'. Christians are quite comfortable with the sounds, smells and atmosphere of church. The church has spent a lot of money on their home grounds. The cloistered comforts of church buildings can lull us into a sleepy apathy. An 'us and them' attitude is cultivated. Christians can get so busy developing church programmes, like many prison teams; they are trapped in a gilded cage and not allowed or encouraged to 'play-away'. But if you are not part of a religious culture, entering a church can be a huge barrier with its strange people, strange smells and strange atmosphere, all of which lend themselves to distraction and intimidation.

As familiar, comfortable and convenient as church can be we have been given a mandate: **'go'**. Sports ministry helps us to 'go', to build relationships with others outside the Christian ghetto; sport helps us enter the opponent's coliseum and play hardball. A recurring theme I hear in seminars around the world is, **'I am so busy doing church work I do not know anybody outside the church.'** But if you are involved in sport you will most certainly know many outside the church and have wonderful shared experiences which will give you a healthy platform from which you can express your faith. We'll give you ideas on how to play away in chapter 11.

Sports Ministry Helps you Focus!

Media corporations used to think in terms of 'broad casting' providing a communications and entertainment resource for a mass appeal; a show had to be all things to all people.

SPORTS OUTREACH

The media trend now is 'narrow-casting', and finding 'Target Audiences' (MTV, cartoon channel, sports channel...). Western audiences are becoming more and more specified and targeted. There are also international trends among youth as the media infiltrates the youth market. The growing reality is the advent of global youth or 'universal adolescents'. A teenager in Poland will have more in common after watching the same television program with a youth in Mexico or Japan. The sports world is a specific target audience with different values and pressures and time constraints. Jesus instructed in Matthew 10: 5-7: *'These twelve Jesus sent out with the following instructions: 'Do not go among the Gentiles or enter any town of the Samaritans. Go rather to the lost sheep of Israel.'* Jesus' instruction seems very uncharacteristic, was Christ only interested in reaching the Jews? Of course not. We see several commands to reach the whole world for Christ. So why such a specific focused group? 1) His disciples were in no way ready to impact Gentiles, this would take a big change of heart, and the guidance and equipping of the Holy Spirit. 2) The Jews had a specific role to play and they were designed to transmit the good news throughout history. We find the Apostle Paul strategically minded as he moves from city to city – we find him first in the synagogue then the marketplace. 3) Jesus was focused. William Barclay writes: 'But the great reason for this command is simply this – **any wise commander knows that he must limit his objectives. He must direct his attack at one chosen point.** If he diffuses his forces here, there and everywhere, he dissipates his strength and invites failure. The smaller the forces, the more limited his objectives must be.' The Apostle Paul in his well-documented three missionary journeys is also single-mindedly focused to best impact the world for Christ. You will see Paul intentionally impacting strategic areas of society, target audiences that were influencing society; whether they are Jewish points of power, centres of commerce or centres of law. God led him to specific centres of influence and he seized them and turned them into Christian centres. Again sport is a target audience and to reach this strategic group takes a determined focus.

Sports Ministry has No Generation Gaps!

I have a photo of a 'Match Day' (see chapter 11 for more on Match-Days) we ran in conjunction with a Billy Graham Crusade in Perth, Scotland. A Match Day is essentially using the atmosphere of a sporting event as the catalyst for creating a responsive formal pre-match gospel presentation. The event was successful and caught the imagination of the Graham Association. What was most exciting was that though we planned on it being a solely youth event it was mixed in ages and sexes. In the photo there is a Grandma, Grandpa, son and grandson all listening to the speaker. Three generations were represented and it did not feel awkward! Why? Because sport transcends the generations and establishes significant relationships. It is a natural point of contact, young people expect adults to show up in the sporting area of their lives. Where many youth workers have to either manufacture points of contact or hover on the fringes of youth culture – sport is a natural point of entry. You don't get that at a pop concert!

Many youth leaders would give their right arm to have access to young people and their world. Margaret Mead's 1970s book *Culture and Commitment* helped create the myth of the generation gap. It was the anthropologist's contention that a radical break had occurred during the 1960s between youth and adults, and that young people would no longer follow adult leadership. In 'Study of Generations', research was done to study whether Mead and other sociologists' contentions were true regarding the Generation Gap. 'The resulting data showed that her much publicized 'generation gap' was true for twenty per cent of the youth population at most. It was a fallacy that youth leaders (and parents) swallowed hook line and sinker.' I feel that this type of misinformation has created an easy excuse to opt out of our investment into our greatest resource – the future. It is no coincidence that a little over one generation on from Mead's book, the Gen X kid feels so unconnected, lost and desiring meaningful relationship – and simultaneously fearful to commitment to meaningful relationships. We want to connect with others but do not know how or are afraid to make the investment. So, in time, we now have arguably two generations with no mentors; the apprentice system is eroding. In the section on 'Reproducing Reproducers' we will deal with this issue in depth (YMTT p.147).

Several factors of strength can be considered in sports ministry. An adult sportsperson has a built-in point of contact with a sporty youth. Natural contact: we are not trying to create opportunities to build relationships, the relationship naturally exists through sport. There is no generation gap in sport; one needs only go to a sporting event to find parent, grandparent and child enjoying a day out together. Likewise a coach-player relationship is quite acceptable within the world of sport. **Whereas most other ministries have to find an entry point of contact, sports ministry has intrinsic bridges.** We will see another recurring theme throughout the New Testament; people are drawn to Christians first, then to Christ. Sports ministry is people; a group that has certain desires, needs, goals and time restraints that easily connect with each other.

SPORTS OUTREACH

Sport the Opiate of the Masses: 'Manchester United is God!'

Seconds after speaking to an evangelistic youth outreach in Manchester a fifteen-year-old boy yelled out in the quiet sports hall: 'Rangers is God!' There was a mixed reaction, some youth were appalled that he would say such a goofy thing, some were offended that he did not mention their own club and a few agreed with him! The leader of the event was embarrassed and pulled the meeting back into order and apologised to me for the outburst. I thought to myself at least his idol (God substitute) was not drugs! A familiar mood amongst youth globally is hopelessness. Why is sexual promiscuity growing even though there is a greater awareness of the risk of sexual diseases? Answer: hopelessness. But this sense of hopelessness is less common in the world of sport (the exception is if you are a Chicago Cubs fan). Karl Marx said, 'religion was the opiate of the masses', sociologists now retort, 'Sports and leisure are the modern opiate of the masses'. Sport is seductive; you can gain self-worth vicariously through your favourite team or your favourite player. Sport has become an acceptable form of idolatry. Though in the long run it is misguided, sport does give hope, direction and a motivation for living.

As recently as forty years ago a preacher would attract an audience by the mere fact that he was an evangelist. Now the modern evangelist has to compete against an array of entertaining media (sport, music, media…) for an audience. It is quite difficult to generate interest in a preacher no matter that they may offer divine truths of eternity. However, if a favourite sports team comes to town, the interest is massive. In just over ten years the Apostle Paul established the church in over four provinces of the Roman Empire. He focused his efforts around three key areas: **unity, institution and culture.** He geared his message towards breaking down the misconceptions people had of God and then communicated a clear gospel in a manner that was comprehensible to the hearer. Could you not see Paul going into the world of sport with the same sadness as he went into Athens? But could you not see Paul seeing the institution of sport as a strategic port to transmit the message of Christ?

While Paul was waiting for them in Athens, he was greatly distressed to see that the city was full of idols. So he reasoned in the synagogue with the Jews and the God-fearing Greeks, as well as in the marketplace day by day with those who happened to be there. A group of Epicurean and Stoic philosophers began to dispute with him. Some of them asked, 'What is this babbler trying to say?' Others remarked, 'He seems to be advocating foreign gods.' They said this because Paul was preaching the good news about Jesus and the resurrection!' ...Paul then stood up in the meeting of the Areopagus and said: 'Men of Athens! I see that in every way you are very religious. For as I walked around and looked carefully at your objects of worship, I even found an altar with this inscription: TO AN UNKNOWN GOD. Now what you worship as something unknown I am going to proclaim to you.

The God who made the world and everything in it is the Lord of heaven and earth and does not live in temples built by hands (Acts 17:17-19, 22-24).

Sport is a 'concentrated centre', a globalized: social organisation of unity, institution and culture. In sports ministry we can embrace this love for sport as a medium to those in that environment, and temper it with biblical truth. 'For while bodily training is of some value, godliness is of value in every way, as it holds promise for the present life as well as for the life to come' (1 Tim. 4:8). We use the momentum of sport to project the message and mission of Christ.

Sport is an Untapped Gold Mine

There is a wealth of untapped resources within the Christian sports community. Again, in a church, it is easy to find a role for a retired piano teacher or organist. A retired javelin thrower might not seem as easy! People are often glad to have an athlete attend their faith community but are at a loss on how to best utilise them. **And yet the athlete can speak the language and have a sphere of influence to a huge and mostly unreached people group.** A sportsperson can also contribute a variety of spiritual principles needed in a church including: assertiveness, discipline, ability to focus under pressure, goal-setting and team-work skills.

Sports ministry is also volunteer intensive, an important characteristic in the world of financial budgets. We have a natural 'tent-maker' in the local sportsperson. Faith communities need to be inclusive. We learn from and interact with each other. Culturally diverse groups are okay until we start saying that one subgroup is right and more valued or more spiritual than your subgroup. We need to hold tight to churches that allow and applaud the uniqueness of their members.

Sports Ministry 'Shapes Culture'

Bob Briner, formerly an American television producer in professional sports, in his brilliant and highly recommended book *Roaring Lambs* writes that society needs to make a resolute effort to be salt and light in 'culture-shaping' arenas of society. Below he contrasts the effect Christ has had on the world of sport in the United States where there has been a concerted effort to reach that specific market for Christ, in contrast to the world of media that we as Christians have, for the most part of the last three decades, abandoned. Briner writes:

'I've spent a good deal of my professional career in two arenas: professional sports and television. I may be biased, but I don't think you could name two more influential fields. From highly visible athletes to a steady stream of programming into your homes, these two fields are truly culture shaping. And they illustrate both the best and the worst of Christian involvement in the world. Certainly, anyone following big-time sports in America is well aware of its problems. Dishonesty, exploitation, drugs, illicit sex, ego gratification gone out of control, and the attempt to deify money are all very significant problems not only for professional sports but also for college sports and, in some communities, even high school sports... However, with all its problems, there is a Christian presence within organized sports that makes life in that community more interesting, dynamic, and meaningful than in many professional communities.

This is because Christians made a deliberate, strategic decision years ago to actively and effectively infiltrate that community with the salt of the Gospel. More than in any other area of American life, Christians are providing salt in almost every activity involving sport... There is almost no athletic gathering of any kind without a significant Christian component... The reason why Christian faith is present in the sports community is that Christians did not run away the minute alcohol was served in a stadium, when games were played on Sunday, when gambling entered the picture. Instead they reasoned that because some of the troubling elements were a part of sports, that was all the more reason for Christians to stay and add as much salt as possible... The contrast between sports and television can hardly be greater. In sports you meet Christians everywhere you go. In more than twenty years of working in television, I have met almost no openly confessing Christian working in mainstream television. The difference in the two communities can hardly be more pronounced. In sports, active Christians provide a life-enhancing seasoning just not present in television. Is it any wonder, then, that most of what is available on our home screens is so lacking in Judeo-Christian content? How can these television people be expected to accurately portray Christian values on the screen if there aren't any Christian producers, screen-writers, cameramen, or directors?

He goes on to say:
Our job as Christians is not to take over the various communities in our world; it is, however, to penetrate them, to be present, to provide God's alternatives to evil, to demonstrate Christ's relevance there, to be as good a representative as possible for Him and His church.

Cautions of Sports Ministry

There are several inherent challenges to an effective sports ministry. Being aware and sensitive to these issues will help you develop a holistic approach. The sports ministers' purpose is no different to any other healthy evangelical ministry: to assist the church in the Great Commission – to win, build, send.

Past mistakes:

- No cohesive, long-term plans for assimilating sports people into the church.
- Not considering the long-term investment it would take to sustain a strategic ministry.
- No attainable goal setting to help the ministry stay on course.
- The programme emphasis erodes from helping people grow in Christ to merely winning competitions.
- Not developing a proper infrastructure for sustainable ministry.
- Not adequately training your leaders or cultivating new leadership.
- Not casting a strategic vision to the church corporately.
- Getting involved in ministry for the wrong reasons.

 If any man builds on this foundation using gold, silver, costly stones, wood, hay or straw his work will be shown for what it is, because the Day will bring it to light. It will be revealed with fire, and the fire will test the quality of each man's work (1 Cor. 3:12-13).

Are you Training your Leaders?

Sports ministry is a vocation for a relatively few full-timers, it is mostly a sideline for volunteers. In volunteer-intensive ministry the quality is only as good as your local volunteer. I have noticed that many sports ministries around the world can be spiritually shallow. It is therefore important to remember that the quality of training will have direct bearing on the quality of ministry. Because sports ministry is relatively new it can be difficult to visualize. There are few quality models out there. It is not uncommon to find a church that has had some sports ministry experience but no clear plan or long-term strategy. A sports ministry is run poorly when the ministry is not a cohesive, well thought out, long-term sports ministry programme. We are a kinetic, proactive bunch – we see a need and move fast. But our strategic thinking and spiritual training can be wanting. For this reason, conferences, training materials and dialogue are important. Doing behind-the-scenes groundwork, creating a strong biblical foundation and building your leaders are not glamorous tasks but the results are longer lasting. You will sacrifice a lot of time and effort, will your effort last or will it be wood, hay and straw?

- Am I building into the lives of my leaders?
- Does my ministry have a long-term projection?
- Am I building a sports ministry on a biblical foundation?

SPORTS OUTREACH

Is your Church Behind You?

Sports ministry is a part of the big picture, not an end to itself. Sports ministry should not be perceived as a full-service ministry but as a focused extension of the general ministry of the church. It is easy to identify with like-minded people; the difficulty lies in integrating sports people into the general life of the church. Sadly there will be unconscious and sometimes conscious reluctance to embracing the sports world. We need to prepare our faith community; if your leaders are reluctant you will have little chance of incorporation. It saddens and frustrates me to see so many talent-laden churches so far away from their remit, and to see Christians unfulfilled because the church is for one reason or another reluctant to fulfil her purpose.

- If you are not sports-minded, recognising the validity and importance of sports ministry is difficult.
    - Does your congregation know its function as a **win, build, send** community?
    - Will your church be encouraged to see the church interrelate?
- Because the church has ignored sports people and the sports arena there are very few sports people in leadership, therefore sports ministry can be subtly marginalized.
    - Is the leadership in your church serious about reaching the sports world for Christ, or merely offering a superficial-perfunctory role within the church's sphere of activity?
- Sports people can be seen to be a nuisance (sometimes rightfully so), if you are not sporty you will not appreciate sport or the strategic importance that sports ministry can play in reaching your community.
    - Can you cast a vision for a role sports ministry can use effectively to reach your communities for Christ? (See Appendix 2)

Don't give up on the church. We resist change for a number of reasons, building the church is costly but strategic. You need to help the local body of believers understand their God-given identity in order to begin living and functioning accordingly and enjoying their identity as fully committed followers of Christ.

Do you Recognise your Weaknesses?

The nature of an athlete lends itself to many characteristics that are conducive to Christian values: team work, discipline, mental-toughness, joy... But there are many characteristics intrinsic to athletes that conflict with Christian faith: self-sufficiency, win at all cost, narcissism... These negative characteristics need to be recognised for what they are and rooted out of our lives.

- Have you given much thought to what a Christian sports culture would look like?
- Are there people in your life that are not afraid to confront you when you step outside biblical boundaries?
    - 'As iron sharpens iron, so one man sharpens another' (Prov. 27:17).

Examine your Motives:

I have heard that if you wait until your motives are perfect to start ministry you will never start. But the purer your motives, the purer your ministry, and in the long term the less impurities you will have to root out of your ministry. The sports world is attractive and can be seductive. You can easily be seduced when your self-worth is vicariously attached to the people you are working with. Often you find people involved in sports-ministry that would bend over backwards to help a professional athlete; would they be as obliging to a street person? Getting involved in ministry to sports people can seem glamorous but the veneer soon fades and becomes hard work. Ask yourself and your leaders:

- Would I make the same effort to serve people that are not high-profile athletes?
- Does working with high-profile athletes make me feel important?
- Do I try to impress others with my ministry – do I like the recognition?
- Is my ministry encouraging others to get involved in serving the local church?
- Do I try to impress youth with my athletic talent?
- Is it important to me to be admired?
- Am I involved in sports ministry because it is the only way my wife will let me participate in sport – if it is in the church!

In the following chapters we will examine the roles of sport, church and ministry strategy. Unless your ministry has a biblical foundation it will be wood, hay and straw: it will not last. In the next chapter we will see how sports ministry has ebbed and waned throughout history.

CHAPTER TWO
HISTORY

WE MADE THE BALL

We All Know How to Play!

COULD there ever have been a point in history when children did not play? A child entering this world has little to offer: they have no language, no ideas and no customs. But you do not need to teach an average baby to play. Play is spontaneous and a gift from God. Homo Luden: man is defined by play. Play helps us expand our physical and defined space. It is a universal phenomenon. Every ancient culture has reflected a form of play and competition. Play helps children acquire motor skills, and helps the social and psychological development. Sport is an institutionalised (in varied degrees) manifestation of play. Society's and culture's function is to create an external environment that is safe and secure. As societies develop a unique phenomenon occurs – 'discretionary time'. With this time came a thirst for recreation (to recreate) and leisure activities. Aristotle said, 'too much activity makes you a beast and not enough makes you effeminate'. We can only imagine what sport would be like in the Garden of Eden (Hebrew: paradise). Man indeed was created to work (Homo Faber) but we see from the 'fall' that work became harder, 'less time'. Before the 'fall', there was no sin, disease or death. When I hear of the possibilities for the human brain, the potential in biomechanics that we have not yet reached, I wonder how fast Adam could run? We will strive to break records as man has still the impulse to be in Eden and to

SPORTS OUTREACH

reflect God's glory. Arthur F Holmes wrote in *Christian Scholars review*, 'Towards a Christian Play Ethic': 'Calvin calls the world the theatre of God's glory. So perhaps Shakespeare was right, and all we men and women are merely players, playing our many parts for God's pleasure and honour. The chief end of man, according to the Westminster divines, is to glorify God and enjoy him forever. Life then is celebration.'

 ## Religion and sport – nothing new

A young athlete feels his pulse quicken and his stomach tighten as he enters into the arena. He hears the crowds cheering and booing and feels faint as he gets a first look at his opponent. A surge of adrenaline rushes to his brain and focuses on the competition and giving glory to his god. Is this the picture of a modern youth walking into a national stadium for sports competition? No, this is a youth from Athens seven hundred years before the birth of Christ competing for the glory of Zeus in the ancient Olympic games. Though the ancient Greek religion is complex and often contradictory, the Greeks understood that man was a multidimensional being including mind, body and soul.

Our oldest association of sport and religion is the ancient Olympic games. Other cities besides Olympia held competitions for their own gods including Delphi, in honour of Apollo, and Corinth and Nemea. Historically athletes such as Thagenes would travel to these four competitions and, like the equivalent of the modern day 'Grand Slam', win all four. Interestingly, the rewards and accolades were materially profitable, betraying the myth of the 'pure amateur athlete' upheld by many in the nineteenth century.

Sport reflected society, most Greek cities loved the body and were proud of their gymnasiums, where men would compete and train in the nude. I bet Adidas and Nike would have hated it!

Rome had a more military emphasis, which promoted boxing, javelin and discus. But the big two sports that were predominantly spectator orientated were gladiatorial games and chariot races which would have over 200,000 spectators. As Rome over three centuries was slowly Christianised we see some of the first examples of Christian influence over sport. As, for example, the Gladiatorial games were scorned and eventually abandoned because of the inhumane brutality and idolatry that surrounded the competition.

Team Sports

Sport was recorded in ancient Egypt during both the time of Joseph and Moses. Egyptian leaders would prove themselves in feats of strength, forms of combat and ball games. Imagine Joseph introducing his brothers to exciting Egyptian sports and Moses in Pharaoh's court learning to ride, race and dual.

Much of sport in the middle ages was emerging sporadically and was loosely organised. Folk-football (a no-holds-barred form of football/soccer) developed, with a game lasting all day and the rules made up as they went along. The competition was generally against a local rival village (one goal in each village) and centred on holidays and festivals. If you have ever been in a tug-of-war in a village fête you will understand the atmosphere of the game. Sport has always been influenced by class distinction and discretionary time. If you had 'leisure time' you could enjoy sport; if you were too busy surviving, there was no time or energy for frivolity. The exception was the soldier; we see commanders of great armies always interested in occupying their men's time when not in combat. The most injuries recorded in the US Army during the Gulf War were received during intramural sports. In the middle ages a knight would joust competitively reflecting again the art of war. These tournaments were lucrative in prize money and reputation. The jousting tournaments evolved more into choreographed exhibitions than true competitions, but in 1559 Henry II was recorded as mortally wounded by a blow from a lance.

In the Renaissance and modern period you see a philosophic East – West split in the approach to sport. The East took on a less confrontational, 'non-competitive' approach to sport, which developed into the presentational sports like gymnastics and evolved into the arts like ballet. And the Western sport took on a more combative style involving teams.

No Bull Dogs

With the Reformation came a renewed emphasis on universal education under church control. This waned and ebbed under Henry VIII, but slowly in the reformed countries of Europe, schools were emerging. The Puritans started to make their mark on society with a heightened emphasis on education; with the Puritanical dispersion a wave of European influence hit the Americas and other colonisations spread to the New Worlds. A renewed emphasis in the Catholic countries also arose due to the 'Counter Reformation' – they also established new schools. Christians again had an influence on sport and society as the Puritans discouraged 'bull-baiting' (breeding powerful dogs for fighting with bulls) and stick fighting which gave way eventually to more organised sport.

Picked Up the Ball

As sport developed into the nineteenth century the ideology of athleticism – 'muscular Christianity' – greatly influenced the independent school. The public (private) school was enjoyed mainly by those privileged enough to have a means to good schooling, which employed the newly established culture of physical education. As the Victorian age developed, three components emerged that shaped the world and catapulted sport into the global culture. Europe and America **industrialized**, **imperialised** and **evangelised**. Big factories needing lots of people developed big cities. Factories needed raw goods that other foreign countries could provide; so big countries influenced, assimilated, educated and controlled small countries. Simultaneously there was a heightened awareness of a world that knew no gospel, and a surge of missionary endeavours scoured the planet bringing with them, of all things, strange balls and bats. The modernization is seen as a time of coercion but many in the newly developing countries were happy to adopt components of Western culture. But modernizers and missionaries also used the power of sport for manipulative purposes suppressing indigenous activities and sports with their own. Many new colonies formed and life centred around the church and school. These two institutions had the dubious responsibility of ensuring that any deculturation did not occur, they were agents of Western preservation, which identified sport as an important cultural heritage. Very few indigenous sports remain for example; though the Olympic Games are global Judo is one of a few non-Western sports represented.

Carried the Ball

Sport was seen at home and abroad as an important agent of moral discipline. From the Victorian era and the Industrial Revolution we see a heightened spiritual and social emphasis, along with urban and industrial changes. Both basketball and volleyball (see side bar on the YMCA and James Naismith) are direct products of the church reaching the unchurched and building the church. Participating in sport was seen as an emulation of the values like fair play, discipline and teamwork. Churches and Christian societies – notably the Young Men's Christian Association – recognised the value of sport and developed it for a worldwide emerging market – factory youth. **Sport has an effect, which instils confidence, pride and unification;** the muscular Christian created exercises and games aimed at ensuring the youth's physical development, while at the same time promoting a wellbeing, which developed sound moral attitudes. These sports needed to be inexpensive and keep the youth off the street. Their new youthful clientele in the industrial age were working merely twelve-hour days in the factories and had too much free time on their hands. Sport became the solution.

Dr James Naismith and the birth of a sport for Jesus

Dr James Naismith's calling to the ministry directed him not to the pulpit but the basketball court. Originally a rural farm boy from Ontario, Canada, of Scottish origins, Naismith planned to become a minister, taking a degree in theology. He was an all-round sportsman with special talent as a gymnast. But it was his idea that sports would teach Christian living that moulded his life. He went to the United States and entered the YMCA School in Springfield, Massachusetts as a member of the sports staff. He was challenged to devise a game that would be conducive to indoor sport because of the brutal New England winters. Sport for Naismith was not merely an activity but food for nurturing the spirit. He understood that sport could build character and that the opportunities learned in sport would shape the athlete and be transferred into the rest of their Christian life.

In December of 1891, at the age of 29, Naismith mounted two peach baskets on poles, divided students into two teams of nine each, (there were eighteen in his class), tossed them a soccer ball and the immensely popular game of basketball was started. It evolved over time (originally there was no hole in the peach basket for the ball to fall through!) and eventually a hoop and net replaced the peach baskets and by 1895 it was standardised with five players a side.

Soon after the turn of the century, the sport had a meteoric rise in popularity at both high school and college level in the States. Naismith's attitude towards the game may have been naïve if we look back from a modern perspective. He said: 'you don't coach basketball, you just play it.'

Although Naismith never became a church pastor, his influence was huge. His main interest was never in basketball itself, but in the Christian lives of those who played it – 'it was not what the boy did with the ball that really mattered, but what the ball did to the boy'. Naismith lived an exemplary Christian life and modelled Christianity to the boys he worked with.

Dr Naismith may not have intended to go into sports ministry but the changing attitude of sport and culture were a good reflection of changing society in late nineteenth and early twentieth century. Sport was catching the imagination of several Christian leaders who wanted to build a strong Christian ethos into both individual and society.

Ran with the Ball

Ironically, with this revitalised emphasis on a Christian society, Christian leaders feeling the responsibility for the blight that industry had brought to the modern city shifted the emphasis for education from church-based to state-based schooling. Many of these reformers brought about legislative change, which would better promote the Christian idea of society. With a new emphasis on universal education came the conviction that sport was the answer for a balanced academic life. These new non-fee-paying schools rigorously emphasised literacy, mental discipline, good moral character and sportsmanship – all qualities used to both evangelise and imperialise the world. Interestingly, as European society was putting the responsibility of education firmly in the lap of the State, it was rushing to create new church-based schools around the world. The missionary movement would not replace the Bible as the cornerstone of truth, but they understood this new and growing phenomenon of organised sport was helpful to underscore its value and transmission of Christian ethics.

Many of the fee-paying independent schools with a strong history of sport would be the training grounds for the new wave of missionary who carried both the Bible and sport globally. International Christian seminaries and teacher training colleges intent on 'reaching the demoralised, influentially corrupt societies, and reforming the hearts of youth', were sprouting from missionary agencies around the world. There were not enough missionaries, teachers and administrators being trained to meet the demand of global modernisation and the fee-paying schools saw themselves as factories for leaders, teachers and missionaries. These new leaders to the new world, brought, for good and bad, their old values, their old culture, old language, old nationalistic sentiments and old leisure pursuits.

Enter, the Pro

Western culture was on the move; modernizers were building and exporting steamships, telegraph lines and modern weaponry as well as football, rowing, athletics, tennis, baseball, cricket and golf. From the primordial soup of organised sport a new creature evolved: the professional athlete. Forces driving men to strive in performance, to win and also to capitalise on the entertainment value took root. This went against the grain of the original organisers of sport, many churches and academic institutions perceived this as a threat to pure sportsmanship. Because professional sport diverged somewhat from the ideal ethos of the amateur, we find the church renouncing its role and influence on the sports world.

Sport is powerful and the churches could not keep the new evolving phenomenon focused on its original purpose. The motives and methods on which sport was originally exported were slowly eroded. Sport turned into its own culture, adapting its own creeds and rhetoric, and making its own aims seem superior. The church was appalled with its creation and for the most part washed its hands of the world of sport, abdicating another culture-shaping arena. Sport is now entrenched into the global fabric. Sport has become part of politics, economics and culture. An athletic image is as useful to a modern corporation as an actor or model. Sport sells.

Engaged – Disengaged – Engaged

In Tony Ladd and Jim Mathisen's book *Muscular Christianity* you can see the influence of the church in developing sport, then turning its back on sport and later re-engaging in sport. Ironically the cultural influence of sport is now stronger in many areas of the world than the church, which gave sport original credibility.

> *When sport moved in increasingly secular directions in the early twentieth century, Protestants moved accordingly—but in two separate directions. While mainline Protestants continued to endorse sport apart from its value for conversion, fundamentalists grew increasingly suspicious of sport and minimized its value. The 150-year interaction between evangelicals and athletes has not always been cordial.' For example, 'Pitcher-turned-evangelist Billy Sunday left professional baseball in part because of the culture of the profession. It wasn't until after World War II, when sport redefined its niche as part of the American way of life, that evangelicals re-established their ties to sport.* **Jim Mathisen and Tony Ladd**

Athletes were seen as pious heroes if they laid down their sport for more wholesome church activities. These attitudes are changing as the church recognises that God gives us all unique gifts to use for His Kingdom. But there are some areas of the world that still need to thoughtfully consider the role of sport in the church. There can be a danger to treat an athlete's endowed gifts as being second-class spiritual talents or over-emphasising an athlete as a marketing tool for God.

In the past twenty years we have seen worldwide expansion ('re-engagement') of sports ministry. In many cultures there is now a foundation or emerging foundation to reach the world of sport for Christ. This trend is arguably influenced from a concerted effort made by a few dedicated ministries who have worked tirelessly over the past fifty years. The universal message by people in sports ministry is that sport is good and a gift from God to be used for God's glory, and Christians in sport are to employ these spiritual gifts in their world.

Lessons to Learn:

Historically, we can learn good lessons for sports ministry. Examine the evolution of sport as it travels through history, intertwining and entrenching itself into almost every global culture. See the power it has to build relationships both interculturally and individually. Remember the transmission of sport was in many quarters an earnest proponent for bettering society and spreading the gospel. Notice that sport remains, but the message of the gospel in many parts of the world is gone. Sport is powerful and seductive and those involved in sport, if not careful, can lose their perspective. Like all God-given attributes: when a good-thing becomes a god-thing it becomes a bad-thing. Sport can quickly become an idol. Many church leaders are fed up with their own sports ministry initiatives: 'I never see these guys in my church and all it does is take some of my leaders away from church or family responsibilities. Worse they wear our names on their shirts, act like jerks in the community sports leagues and give us a bad name!'

Sport is great and has loads of potential but because of its power it can become a God-substitute in your life and ministry if not kept in check. A gift that spoils instead of enhances. But isn't that our lifelong struggle – to keep God at the top of our life— to submit to our Lord and pray: 'your kingdom come your will be done'. God has endowed us with all we need to develop a strong ministry. **Biblical Truth**: which gives us direction and purpose. **Reason**: which gives us the capacity to examine truth and motives. **Will**: which gives us the ability to choose right or wrong. **History**: to see vicariously the success and mistakes of others. **Creativity**: to take what we were given and invest into the Kingdom of God. And even better: **Salvation** through Jesus: to give us freedom to act, and the **Holy Spirit** to illuminate us, to better see the big picture. What more do we need to impact the world for Christ?

CHAPTER THREE
BIBLICAL FOUNDATIONS

GOD'S GAME PLAN

Oh, that their hearts would be inclined to fear me and keep all my commands always, so that it might go well with them and their children forever! **(Deut. 6:29)**.

A bible which is falling apart usually belongs to someone who is not. C H Spurgeon

Mighty in the Scriptures:

ISN'T it great that God left us with a book: a 'game-plan' for life! The building of the individual and corporate life of the local church must have its foundation firmly in the Bible. This section is an examination of how biblical principles must nurture, guide and create a solid sports ministry foundation. This may seem a simple principle, but in reality it is a hard practice. Sadly, many well-intentioned people start sports ministry from the paradigm of sport first and then try to relate it to the Scriptures. God did not spin out this world and then retreat. He is active and desires our obedience. Neither did He leave us without guidance and direction. I hope this is a challenge to you to love and read and absorb God's Word. You shouldn't take to the playing fields, courts, rinks or rings without confidence and a desire to do your best. Neither should you go into ministry lightly. Dive into Scripture the way you would enter competition. Acts 18:24: 'Now a certain Jew named Apollos, an Alexandrian by birth, an eloquent man, came to Ephesus and was mighty in the scriptures.' Be like Apollos: 'mighty in the scriptures'.

If you are new in your faith or have never been challenged to enjoy the Bible it may seem intimidating. Do not worry about that, you are not alone. Start now – fall in love with the Bible. Chuck Swindoll said, 'Read your scriptures until your blood turns bibline' – your life will be richer and your depth of being, mentally, physically, socially and spiritually will be more abundant. God's Word is God's way to know Him. I have asked several Biblical Scholars if they feel they have now completely mastered the Scripture, the question to them seems ludicrous! 'Of course not,' is the common answer, 'God is continuously teaching me more of His sufficiency and power'.

Scripture keeps you on track and within the boundaries of life. If you are called to leadership you are called to knowing God. God gave us this book and every word is there with purpose and power.

My son, preserve sound judgment and discernment, do not let them out of your sight; they will be life for you, an ornament to grace your neck. Then you will go on your way in safety, and your foot will not stumble (**Prov. 3:21-23**).

God's Word – the Scriptures – contains: His Message, His instructions, His biography, His promises, His purposes.

You may buy a Bible but you do not own it until the author owns you.
Navigator's Dictum

There are sixty-six separate books of the Bible. They were written originally in three languages: Hebrew, Greek and Aramaic. The books are unique and serve different purposes but with complete synergy. There are: poetry, memoirs, letters, travel, diaries, legal documents, encouragements, admonishments, inventories, polling statistics, family trees.

How to Study God's Word?

We read the Bible for protection and to mount an offensive in spiritual warfare. Note that Christ always used Scripture when He was tempted and or was refuting Satan. 'The tempter came to him and said, "If you are the Son of God, tell these stones to become bread." Jesus answered, "It is written: 'Man does not live on bread alone, but on every word that comes from the mouth of God'"' (Matt. 4:3-4).

Your local Christian bookstore will have a proliferation of Bibles, good modern translations and Bible-guides to help you study. A key to bible study is consistency. Read your Scriptures with a plan and stick to it. After you have achieved some goals, (perhaps reading the Bible in a year) do something different and fresh, but be consistent and systematic. The old Bible college story goes: Imagine the guy who zipped through the pages, stopped and popped his finger down on a verse saying, 'God, whatever the scripture says – I will obey!' He looks down and the Scripture is from Matthew 27:5 'Then (Judas) went out and hanged himself!' 'Oh God perhaps I got it wrong let me try again'. He zips through the Bible and pops his finger down and reads Luke 10:37: 'Jesus told him, "Go and do likewise".'

When you read the Bible the questions below will help give you perspective. Also remember that Jesus gave you the Holy Spirit and that He will guide you and open up the Scriptures in a special way.

- Ask God to help you understand what is being said.
- Ask yourself:
  - Who is being addressed?
    Is this for a group of small house churches in Rome?
    Is this a love letter to God?
    Is this a chronicle of a great nation?
  - Who is speaking – who are these people?
    Are they kings or slaves?
    Are they about to go to war?
    Are they poor or living in luxury?
  - Where are they?
    Is this an intimate prayer in a garden?
    Is this a sermon on a mountain?
    Is this a letter written from jail?
  - What is the purpose of this address?
    Is this a rally cry to encourage soldiers?
    Is this a reply to hostile religious men?
    Are these instructions on how to share your faith?
  - How do these Scriptures apply to me?
    How can I love my neighbour today?
    How can I stay humble and yet play confidently?

- What words can I speak that will encourage my team-mates?

Theology:

What is theology? On the Oxford University coat of arms is the inscription 'Dominus illuminatio mea' – the Lord is my light. C S Lewis, an Oxford Professor, wrote: 'I believe in Christianity as I believe the sun has risen, not only because I see it but because by it I see

SPORTS OUTREACH

everything else.' God has given us a guide that is specifically opened to us under the power, 'illumination', of the Holy Spirit. The Bible is not an exhaustive book of information, though it speaks of 'sowing' and 'harvesting' it does not give me specific information on how to care for my geraniums. Likewise, the Bible does not give me coaching techniques on how to teach my son to play soccer but it does give me clear direction on what my attitude should be whilst coaching him ('Fathers, do not aggravate [embitter] your children. If you do they will become discouraged and quit trying ' (Col. 3:21 NLT). Our aim as Christians is to respond as best we can, in our belief system to reflect and hold fast to God's divine Word. That is good theology.

J I Packer in *Concise Theology* says:
As an activity theology is a cats cradle of interrelated yet distinct disciplines:

- Elucidating texts (exegesis)
- Synthesizing what they say on the things they deal with (biblical theology)
- Seeing how the faith was stated in the past (historical theology)
- Formulating it for today (systematic theology)
- Finding its implications for conduct (ethics)
- Commending and defending it as truth and wisdom (apologetics)
- Defining the Christian task in the world (missiology)
- Stockpiling resources for life in Christ (spirituality)
- Corporate worship (liturgy)
- Exploring ministry (practical theology)

God teaches us that we need to develop a good base on which to build our ministry. We reflect and internalise the Bible then act on that reflection. Much like how an athlete first receives coaching, and then performs. If the coaching is sound, the performance will be sound, when adhering to the instruction and according to ability. Therefore dodgy theology, like dodgy coaching (I used to be encouraged not to drink water because it would make me tough, it almost killed me!), is dangerous. Don't get psyched-out by the word theology. If you have participated in sport long enough, I believe you can be a great theologian! You have taken a multiplicity of interrelated disciplines and fused them into action. That is all theology is – taking God's game plan and living it.

God's Game Plan:

1. It gives us purpose.
2. It gives us direction.
3. It gives us focus.
4. It gives us energy.
5. It gives us safety.

We all have our prejudices and need a compass system to navigate our sport, lives and society. God gave us the 'true north', a map, a compass and a guide. Volumes have been written about theology. We can learn much from studying mankind, his origins, intention, his fall, his redemption and his Commission – more than can be synthesised and examined in this book. For the best thinking on sport and theology I want to direct you to Stuart Weir's book *What the Book says about Sport*. In it he examines the Scriptures as a theologian and the implications they have for us in the world of sport. For over a decade the Christians in Sport staff has knocked around, built and torn down, projected and learned and borrowed theological principles that seemed to pertain directly to sport. Stuart has distilled these thoughts into a palatable and encouraging book. He made it look easy!

What is the Gospel we Proclaim?

Our answer lies in the Scriptures.

> *Then Jesus came to them and said, 'All authority in heaven and on earth has been given to me. Therefore make disciples of all nations, baptizing them in the name of the father and of the son and of the Holy Spirit, and teaching them to obey everything I have commanded you. And surely I am with you always, to the very end of the age'* **(Matt. 28:18-20).**

Let us examine a few of these principles:

Mankind:
- Man is the most important part of the created order (Gen. 1 & 2)
    - Man is valued highly, more than sparrows. The act of redemption declares man of infinite worth (Matt. 10:29)
- Man was made in likeness, image. Godlike but not God (Gen. 1:26-27)
    - Because of this special endowment man is worthy of honour and respect.
- Superior to nature, though used part of existing material from nature (dust) to create him (Gen. 2:7)
    - Man was given authority and work (Gen. 2:15)
    - Throughout the OT the relationship of man and nature is stressed. Nature was made to serve man; man was made to tend nature.
    - Man was also given volition, choice to stay within boundaries and capability to sin, to break the boundaries (Gen. 2:16-17)
- God creates two institutions, which teach one to live under authority and to live for someone other than himself (Gen. 2:17-27)
    - law
    - marriage

- Man is intimately known – every hair on your head is numbered (Matt. 10:30)
  - As a creature, man is expected to obey the ordinances of God (Matt. 19:3)
  - Man's mind and conscience extends over the whole activity of his being (Col. 2:18)

Consequences of sin:

- Through Adam's sin we have inherited this disease/death incurable by man (Rom. 6:23)
- The basic meaning of sin is failure to hit the mark.
  - We keep breaking the rules and going out of bounds (trespass)
  - The disease is universal to man with no exemptions (Rom. 3:23)
  - The disease is internal, with external outcomes. The bad on the inside causes bad on the outside (Gen. 3:23)
  - The implication of this sin is separation from God (Rom. 6:23)
  - And the consequences for separation from God are condemnation and hell (Matt. 23:33)

God's Grace:

- God is a gracious God
  - Grace: unmerited favour (Rom. 5)
  - God demonstrates his love for us in this, while we were yet sinners, Christ died for us (Rom. 5:8)
- He enjoys His creation and takes pleasure in its obedience, praise, and acknowledgement (John 14:15)
- God is intimate with His creation and values us beyond finite expression (1 John 3:1)
- God's creation has no strength or merit in him to redeem himself (Prov. 10:16)
- But God in His sovereignty unfolded His plan for redemption to us by sacrificing His Son and transferring the guilt onto Christ (John 19:30)
- Christ is the cure.
  - We were bought with blood. God's Son Jesus redeemed us with His own life (John 3:13-18)
  - We have been sealed by the Holy Spirit (Eph. 1:13)
  - Salvation is by Jesus dying for us and living in us (John 15:4)
  - Access to this salvation come in the vital union which is sustained by the Spirit on God's side and by faith from our side which is formed and in our new birth.
  - Sinners are saved from sin and death but what are they saved for?

- To love God: Father, Son and Holy Spirit, in time and eternity (Matt. 22:37)
- Next, to love our neighbour (Matt. 22:37)

God's purpose:

- We have an ongoing transformation – becoming what God has intended us to be (Rom. 12:1-2)
  - Regeneration is birth, transformation is growth (1 Cor. 6:9-11)
  - God's people are given gifts (tools) for works of service, so that the Christ body (corporation) may be built up (Eph. 4:7-12)
  - We have been adopted into God's family to enjoy the rich inheritance and responsibilities that come with the title (Rom. 8:17). We bear His character and His redemptive purposes.

Our Commission:

- God has lavished on us this remarkable and unthinkable love that
  - forgives us (Acts 2:38)
  - cleans us (Heb. 9:22)
  - gives us,
    - riches (Eph. 2:7)
    - unique gifts (Matt. 7:11)
    - purposes (Ps. 57:2)

- We are to bring glory to God (John 15:8)
  - To glorify acknowledges allegiance and obedience to God.
  - Glory:
    - to extol
    - to attribute praise
    - I can tell my child to sing alleluia but when my child decides to attribute glory to God out of his own understanding and volition then will he truly glorify God
- Glory fulfils function: (Rom. 8:17)
  - We were created our function was to attribute honour.
- How do we attribute Glory
  - Verbally
  - Mentally
  - Physically
  - Socially

SPORTS OUTREACH

- Spiritually
- Submission
  - In obedience
  - Commissioned
  - Mission

What does this mean to me?

From the third chapter of the first book of the Bible, Genesis, we see that God is at odds with man who, through his free will and disobedience, separated himself from God. God, in the rest of the Scriptures, displays His unfailing love and redemptive character for His creation; unfolding His pattern for bringing man back into harmony with Himself. God uses His people for His purposes. He will equip those for service, and service comes in many forms. We have an opportunity to demonstrate God's love with His indwelling presence. We are 'ambassadors' (2 Cor. 5:17-20), 'to preach the good news and proclaim forgiveness.' It is from this biblical foundation that we get our strategy for ministry.

In the movie *Chariots of Fire*, Eric Liddell says, 'I believe God made me for a purpose – for China – but when I run I feel his pleasure and to give it up would be to hold him in contempt. To win is to honour him.' In Stuart Weirs' book, *What the Book Says About Sport* Stuart writes 'According to the Westminster Confession, we were created to glorify God. Is there any reason why that should not be on the sports field just as much as in the church?' All in Christ have been redeemed, adopted and given certain privileges and responsibilities. When I stop and take in the impact of this amazing grace I am compelled to go to my knees in thanks and praise. My guess is I can only fathom the tiniest tip of the iceberg; I grow closer to Christ with the years and comprehend more of God's grace, the breadth, width and depth of God's love for us. Romans 12:1: 'Therefore, I urge you, brothers, in view of God's mercy, to offer your bodies as living sacrifices, holy and pleasing to God – this is your spiritual act of worship.' In Romans 12 we see Paul urging us to understand more of God's mercy, and in response, 'in view of' that great love, to give all to God.

You have nothing to do but save souls. Therefore spend and be spent in this work.
John Wesley

CHAPTER FOUR
FAST TRACK

SHORT CUTS TO
SUCCESSFUL SPORTS MINISTRY

There are no
short cuts
(or are there?)

 Consecration precedes conquest **Chuck Swindoll**

SPORTS OUTREACH

I **WONDER** if you went straight to this section skipping over Efficacy, History and Biblical Foundation? If so I guess two types of people went here first. 1) The type of person that is so appalled that a chapter would even suggest that you could have 'short cuts' in ministry. You came here to criticize this chapter. I want to agree with you but don't be too quick to condemn this chapter; I do have some suggestions that will make your ministry more effective. 2) The type who came here first thinking yes, I don't have to read the whole book! Just give me a few quickie ideas and I am off to win the sports world for Christ, after all I am important and busy! I wish I could give you the keys to success in three thousand words! But it is not that easy, ministry is a long hard slog. Read on!

 If a man cleanses himself from the latter, he will be an instrument (weapon) for noble purposes, made holy, useful to the master and prepared to do any good work (2 Tim. 2:21).

Beating on Trees with Axe Handles

There is no cheap solution to successful sports ministry. But there are ways to be more effective. I remember Tommy Nelson, a Dallas-based pastor who was speaking at my Fellowship of Christian Athletes training week. He said 'I am tired of beating on trees with axe handles' Tommy went on to tell the old story: 'There were two lumber jacks in the woods, one young and strong the other old but wise. The young man started to brag about how many trees he could fell in a day. The older man snorted out a laugh at the young kid's boast. This incensed the youth's pride who replied, "old man what are you laughing at? I could cut down more trees in a day than you could dream of." The old man laughed harder at this ridiculous boast and they decided to make a wager on who could cut down the most trees in a day. The next morning a forestry official looked at his clock and yelled go! The young man flew into the forest and you could hear the crack of the axe echoing through the forest as he attacked each tree. But the old man sauntered off into the tool shed got out a file and started sharpening his axe. At the end of the day the old man had won.'

Whether you are in full-time ministry or coaching five-year-olds once a week, if you want to be in ministry I suggest you keep your axe sharp. You will cut down more trees and your ministry will be more effective. Let me clear the ground on a few issues. **You are called to have a successful ministry.** Some people really resist the idea of success in ministry. I am surprised when we hear people use the missionary who has given their whole life to a certain mission field and never won a single person to Christ as a positive model of ministry. I have never met this missionary and am sure they are enduring but I have to ask were they fruitful? Perhaps they were not skilled in a certain job and should have gotten someone better suited to go in their place. Maybe people resist success because they do not want to be disappointed. Disappoint hurts. But I think I would rather raise my standard and be disappointed rather than lower my standard and go through life doing substandard ministry! Some people in ministry, whether they are leading Sunday school or leading a denomination, should be fired, sacked! If they were doing a secular job they would not have lasted.

I am so glad that the apostles were successful. We would not be here if they weren't. I am so glad that my coach was successful (he led me to Christ). I would not be here, probably in jail, if he was not driven to excellence! Michael Green once told our Christians in Sport staff: 'I never met a fisherman who, coming back after fishing and, when asked how did you do? reply, 'I didn't catch anything but I sure influenced a few'.'

What is Success?

The root word means succession, another generation. Much of this is covered in Chapter 8. But we were called to bless the next generation. I think in many parts of the Western world we enjoyed the fruits of Christianity but never planted and so left the next generation in famine. Will you take the challenge and start being an effective and useful minister?

> **To 'Fast track' is to do your ministry supernaturally, not naturally.**

It will be what you do spiritually that will release power for what you do in your ministry. These skills create short cuts. You can have the best meetings and greatest facilities and the funniest stories, but if you are not accessing these supernatural (spiritual) principles your ministry will be shallow.

There will be dark spiritual forces that will keep you from sharpening your axe. A minister once said, 'Satan works 24 hours a day so why shouldn't I!' He burned-out of ministry and on reflection said, 'What was I doing using the devil for my ministry model!' Something will whisper in your head, 'you don't have time to sharpen your axe, you have too many important things you should be doing!' Do you see the arrogance when you give into that lie? It is saying what you do is important instead of what God commands you to do. Don't beat on trees with axe handles.

SPORTS OUTREACH

Here are some suggestions for keeping the axe sharp:

Success means Faithfulness

Give all you have to God and allow Him to use you. I always find solace in my friend's jovial encouragement. We were sitting on a mountain overlooking Southern California the night before graduation when my friend Bob VanSetten, also a theology student, told me, 'Steve, the Lord can use a rock for ministry and the Lord can use an ass for ministry, he can use you for ministry!' Be faithful and allow our Lord to use you for successful ministry. It is not your skill, it is your faithfulness to Him that will bring success.

Success means Prayer

If God answered all your prayers this week how many new Christians would there be? No, I did not ask you how many aunties would have their hips replaced, I asked you, how many new Christians there would be. This is the easiest way to cure anaemic Christian sports ministries. Just ask yourself how often do the Christians pray for those they want to win for Christ? Bringing people before God is our duty and privilege. 'Those with one mind were continually devoting themselves to prayer' (Acts 1:14). Sometimes it is wonderful, sometimes it is merely work, but it is effective. Christ modelled fervent, undistracted times of prayer. The question begs to be asked: if Jesus needed to spend time in prayer, how much more do we need to? I find having a prayer journal very encouraging. I can look back and see how God is working. I often forget to pray for people that I really want to pray for. But a list with specifics is helpful. Let me encourage you to pray in the morning first thing and, if you are married, never go to sleep without praying together. This has been a rich and vital part of our marriage. Vary your prayers. Mine tend to get rote if I do not change my routine. For instance, we receive many cards during the Christmas season. I love the ones that also enclose a photo of them and/or their families. After the holidays I cut them out and stick them in my Bible. It is a good visual journal of people I want to pray for.

Success means Scripture Intake

This has been mentioned in our chapter on God's game plan. But let me say again that the Scripture is a map to God and His purposes for you. If you want to fast track your ministry you need a map. Do not wander in the wilderness. You will have a lifetime of joy studying God's Word.

Luke 11:28: 'hear and obey'. Ronald Whitney writes in *Spiritual Disciplines*, 'If your growth in Godliness were measured by the quality of your Bible intake, what would be the result?' Are you growing or stunted. Are you applying what you learn? When is the last time you memorized a Scripture verse?

Success means Encouragement

I had initially written fellowship. But the word fellowship does not mean what many of us think any more. If you ask someone if they are getting fellowship they usually respond ya, I am going to church. Fellowship does not mean just being in the proximity of other Christians.

It means being encouraged by other Christians. You can go to church for years, sit in the same pew, be polite with others, and never encourage or be encouraged by others. Encouragement is something to ask God for. Encouragement is also something you really need to **do** and pray that it will return to you. There are seasons in your life that you will have few who can encourage you. Don't retreat from encouraging others. But can I suggest that there are a thousand people out there who want to encourage you. You will have to go to a bookstore to find them. This in no way replaces actual corporal fellowship, but many people who write are called to encourage. Find those authors and they will take you deeper in your faith.

Success means Application

Again this will be covered, but it does not hurt re-emphasizing these points. It is no use just taking in time with God, Scripture, and taking in encouragement without doing something about it. That is why you can develop so much more during the season. In the off-season you can lift, train, run and practise shots. But it is in the actual playing that all these skills come together. You cannot have testimony if you do not have experience. To know about God's provision and to experience it are two different things.

Success means Dreaming and Planning

God will use you. A life submitted to Him is a powerful tool. There are dreamers (visionaries) and planners in this world but they rarely seem to get together. Why not? Get out of your box! The two are compatible. I know some people who have a million good ideas but they are so undisciplined that they never get anything done. On the other hand there are people who are so tied to details that they never ask themselves if they are going in the right direction. Usually sports ministry is a small group, reaching out to a team or league. You do not have the benefit of a fifty-man staff with some assigned to management and others assigned to research and development. You have to learn both skills. Ask God to give you big dreams and then plan out how you can best achieve those dreams. There is a point of give and take. Once, running a sports camp, I was accused by a dream guy, that hated detail, of being 'so organized that I was not allowing the Holy Spirit to work'. I had to ask was not the Holy Spirit guiding us when we made our plans. On the same day I was accused of not sticking to my guns on a certain policy, the policy was not working and hindering our big dream. Both the plans and the dreams kept me in good perspective.

SECTION TWO
FIVE PRINCIPLES OF SPORTS MINISTRY

BIBLICAL FOUNDATIONS
DETERMINE PRINCIPLES

Sports Ministry Principles

- Proclamation: Verbalisation of truth.
- Demonstration: Visualization of truth.
- Maturation: Nourishment of truth.
- Reproduction: Reproducing reproducers.
- Sportsmanship: Encouraging a Christian sports culture.

Principles which determine method:

You can slice the ministry of the church into several different sectors, quarters, divisions and subdivisions. In this section, I want to examine five principles of sports ministry. They are unique but interrelated. You may unconsciously be executing three principles simultaneously whilst focusing on a fourth. Incorporating all of these principles is crucial to the big picture – **making disciples**. Take a close look at the eyewitness accounts of Jesus' ministry. He modelled all five of these principles, building into the lives of His disciples and others. As Robert Coleman has written in his classic book *The Master Plan of Evangelism* 'the book does not seek to interpret specific methods of Jesus in personal or mass evangelism. Rather this is a study in principles underlying his ministry—principles which determined his methods.' Most people gravitate towards one or two principles while shying away from others. Some people are better at 'talking the talk' and others at 'walking the walk'. This section will help you identify and value different aspects of ministry, as well as develop both your strengths and weaknesses. A good soccer player uses both feet. A good basketball player can both shoot and rebound. A good defensive tackle can play the pass and run. And a good (mature) Christian can both proclaim and demonstrate the good news of Jesus Christ. Keeping these principles in perspective and implementing them in your ministry takes skill and balance. Balance comes with a biblical foundation and skill comes with practice, encouragement and training according to your God-given talents.

'But we have this treasure in jars of clay'

I often speak at conferences and give countless seminars on sports ministry – one of my favourite illustrations I call the: 'Priority-factor – filling the jar'. The concept was introduced to me, not from church seminars or the sports world but from the business sector, a book on time management: *First Things First: Coping with the ever-increasing demands of the workplace,* Covey, Merrill & Merrill. For example, speaking recently at the YMCA directors' training day in Glasgow I brought a jar and in front of the group added some large rocks. I could barely fit in five and left the others on the table, I asked 'Is the jar full?' and they all said 'yes'. From behind the table I pulled out a bag of gravel and poured it into the jar. I asked, 'Is it full?' They all nervously laughed, fidgeted in their chairs, looked at their colleagues and wondered what I was getting at? Next I poured sand into the jar and you could watch it trickle down in between the rocks. Again I asked 'Is it full?' There was a bit of a murmur but no one wanted to bite on my 'trick question'! I got another grin when I was able to lastly pour in water over the rocks, gravel and sand. The usual response to the question 'so what is the purpose of the illustration? is 'you can fit more in than you thought'. Well actually the point is: 'if you don't put the big things in first it is harder to get them in later'. My father was a master of loading the boot (trunk) of the car with precision when we would travel. His tip which I still hear ringing in my mind is, 'Stevie you gotta put the big things in first!'

On leaving professional sport and first going into ministry I was amazed at how quickly you could fill your day with things that were on B lists and C lists of effective ministry, hoping somehow the A's would magically materialize in the day. This brilliant illustration has reminded me over and over that if I do not make a concerted effort to implement important things into my life and ministry, they sit on the table while less important things fill the jar of my life. It is hard to pray and read my Bible if I do not make that concerted effort to make them a priority. It is also too easy to let less important things fill my ministry while I let the important things slip away.

How do you get the rocks back in?

The question I am often asked is: 'I am already involved in ministry and sadly these principles are not in my jar, how do I get them in?' It is hard to back up, but retooling can invigorate and add new life to ministry. First you have to really value the 'big things', which are the hard things – if they were easy everyone would be doing them. Second, you have to clearly cast a vision to those whom you are involved with. Don't expect people to follow blindly. Lastly, you have to set aside time to plan for them. Implementing ministry principles does not happen by accident; you have to work hard at it. Starting the process will help you to realign your methods in accordance with your priorities: biblical principles that shape your method.

It takes a lot of energy to build a healthy ministry and keep it on course; I hope examining the next five principles will help you build an intentional and effective sports ministry.

In this swaying postmodern world of boomers, busters and gen-Xers, these five principles are universal, timeless and self-evident.

CHAPTER FIVE
PROCLAMATION

VERBALISATION OF TRUTH

>> *And how can they believe in the one of whom they have not heard? And how can they hear without someone preaching to them? And how can they preach unless they are sent?* **(Rom. 10:14-15).**

>> *Evangelism is one beggar showing another beggar where to find bread.*

>> *Are you fishers of men? Or keepers of fish bowls?* **E.V. Hill**

YOU have been transferred to a new team thousands of miles from home. Not long ago your life was turned right side up by new life in Christ. You have now experienced freedom, joy and the knowledge that everything you had ever done wrong was forgiven. Even better, you realised that the Creator of the universe was on your side – better – you are on His side! You know you have been 'adopted' into God's family, He commands you to address Him now as 'dear Father'. And you have received an inheritance that is beyond your wildest imagination. Don't you just want to tell somebody!

SPORTS OUTREACH

 Are you an evangelist?

As a young Christian, I was once accosted by a cheerless woman (she had a tight bun in her hair that gave her a strange aura of authority) in my new found local church. She asked in a stern condescending tone, in front of all my friends: 'are you doing evangelism at your school?' I hadn't a clue what the word *evangelism* really meant. She could very well have been asking me if I was doing drugs in school or getting good grades, to be honest I was doing neither. Evangelism: I did not like the sound of the word; to me it sounded like a medical term for a terminal disease! Being unchurched I was having difficulty finding Genesis in the Bible, my churchy vocabulary was non-existent. Being put on the spot and not wanting to look stupid I guessed (I thought it was a fifty/fifty chance I would win this lady's favour – why I wanted her favour is still a mystery), with an air of self-confidence and divine inspiration I said, 'Oh ya!'. She looked at me with approving eyes and replied: 'I think you are going to be an evangelist when you grow up'. I thought to myself, 'I don't really know what the heck an evangelist is but I hope not!' Prophets come in all shapes – but mostly odd shapes!

Proclamation – Talking the Talk

Proclaiming God's truth, i.e. evangelism, is arguably the most written about and least practised subject in Christendom: like the fishing club that meets every week and talks about fishing but never actually fishes, or the chap that stirs the paint but never takes it out of the pot. For the purpose of this book I do not want to differentiate ministry from evangelism. Some want to call it sports ministry, others sports evangelism, both are right depending on the agreement that getting rooted into the faith community is an integral part of evangelism and ministry. If you don't believe that, I suggest you try and get your money back for this book! In Michael Green's book *Evangelism through the Local Church* he quotes William Temple,

'To evangelise is so to present Jesus Christ in the power of the Holy Spirit, that men shall come to put their trust in God through him, to accept him as their saviour, and serve him as their King in the fellowship of his church.'

 How beautiful are the feet of those who bring good news! (**Rom. 10:14-15**).

So how beautiful are your feet?

Evangelism: the word is derived from the Greek verb *euangelizomai*, to announce or proclaim good news. We have great news to share and we should love to tell the story. The message is not ours but God's: this message must be clear and our method must be strategic. Communicating these truths is a 'commission' – a direct order from God to all Christians, no one is exempt. A non-proclaiming Christian is a contradiction in terms. Work hard at understanding and communicating the gospel. Realise that when you communicate God's universal truth, powerful forces will emerge to both illuminate and distract the message. This is a good-guy bad-guy war with eternal consequences. *The degree to which we understand, value and give attentiveness to these truths, will be the degree and measure with which we strive to transmit these truths.* We are focused when we realise real people go to heaven and real people go to hell.

 From everyone who has been given much, much will be demanded; and from the one who has been entrusted with much, much more will be asked (**Luke 12:48**).

Do or die

Study after study implies that when the emphasis on evangelism is lost the organisation, whose original intent was to proclaim Christ, will erode, shrink and die. When a Christian loses its way the vitality and function is lost. When ministry shifts from a biblical emphasis on personal salvation to a primary focus on social issues, the organisation cannot reproduce itself. In no way am I implying we should ignore the poor and disenfranchised. Ministry turns its back on social issues at its own peril! In fact, when social issues are neglected a vacuum is created that is usually answered by secular organisations with good motives but misguided solutions. For example, the American Civil Liberties Union (ACLU) though it was around for several years managed to entrenched itself as a champion for civil rights after tackling the race issues. While concurrently, mainline white middle-class churches sat on the sidelines at best and at worst turned their back on equal rights for all races. The ACLU has grown into an antagonist for churches ever since. Social issues are very important, but the solution is, and always will be, in God's plan of redemption. All other quasi-solutions are merely a bandage on a festering cancer.

You may ask: what does this have to do with sports ministry? We need to understand that ministry is first and foremost about God; introducing and cultivating personal salvation through and in obedience to Jesus Christ. **To emphasise anything else creates a disease that enters the fabric of your ministry and society and renders it impotent.** When personal salvation and lordship are devalued, for any reason, the consequences of ministry become ambiguous, confusing, ineffective and frustrating. Statistics maintain that when the church loses its evangelistic edge it dies! Why? Because Jesus' blood is the key to all issues of reform. Social problems are extremely important in the context of salvation and Lordship; Jesus commands us to be attentive to the poor, big time! But it is in Christ and His Kingdom that the answers will be found.

SPORTS OUTREACH

Who's pushing religion?

Are you ashamed of Jesus? It has become a frustrating trend among many youth ministers to shy away from a clear presentation of the gospel. Perhaps it is a knee-jerk response from a methodology that tried to cram Christianity down others' throats. Except possibly for some fringe eccentrics the 'cramming' strategy is thankfully long gone. The Apostle Paul encourages us to: 'Be completely humble and gentle; be patient, bearing with one another in love.' I was on a radio interview for the BBC recently discussing the challenges of living the Christian life as a professional athlete. Halfway through the discussion the interviewer said 'We don't want "religion" pushed at us any more'. I asked him, 'can you give me one example in the past year of someone 'pushing religion' at you?' Over national radio there was a pregnant pause. It is more myth than reality that Western society is oppressed by a heavy-handed version of Christianity. A myth perpetuated by television or the occasional rantings on city streets.

The reality is that we are not proclaiming the gospel enough and we have very few models of people expressing their faith in a fearless, winsome and effective manner. To dispel the myth there need to be opportunities of clear loving proclamation. I often tell my friends who are outside of the church that they should be insulted when those in the church are not telling them about Christ! I get blank looks until I explain, 'you see, you may not believe Jesus is the Saviour who can wipe away your guilt, you may not believe in a literal heaven or hell, you may not believe in the Holy Spirit, but they do believe with all their hearts. It is real for them. Can you imagine that they can keep that to themselves because they are afraid you may reject it or think them a fool? If you had good news that you believe would benefit me forever and did not share it, I would be insulted!' My friends usually are not sure how to take it but they usually are more sympathetic to personal evangelism.

Christianity is not, and never will be, fashionable

If anyone is ashamed of me and my words in this adulterous and sinful generation, the Son of Man will be ashamed of him when he comes in his Father's glory with the holy angels (**Mark 8:38**).

There is a very real internal (spiritual) battle as to whether or not to embrace Christ. The gospel awakens a spiritual desire. We want the cure but not the medicine. I heard once, 'If we make God look bad, sin looks good'. Again Paul says, *'For we are to God the aroma of Christ among those who are being saved and those who are perishing. To the one we are the smell of death; to the other, the fragrance of life' (2 Cor. 2:16).* Many outside the church avert and transfer their inward strife with outward ridicule towards the conveyer of the good news. Because if you do not repent it is actually pretty bad news! Very few people enjoy being ridiculed. In fact those few I know that seem to enjoy being ridiculed are often so caustic they are not effective in sharing their faith. Embarrassment is no fun. So with a little flack we sometimes retreat. We can start to rationalise our position from many different angles. It is easy to pontificate about the glories of Christ in the comforts of the Christian ghetto. I remember speaking at a Christian conference focusing on evangelism. One of the conference delegates started speaking in a strange self-righteous tone about, 'leaving the unwholesome hockey team' so he would 'have more time for the church'. My colleague laid into him! Asking, 'then who would be the salt and light in your hockey team, how will they know about Jesus if you are not there! Isn't that your ministry?' I think Mr Righteous started polishing his boots that night.

Proclamation (expressing the truth of the gospel) is Christianity. To be so captivated with a sense of deliverance from sin by God's Son should radiate from your life and speech. Every single talent you possess is given to you to proclaim and build the Kingdom of God. Utilizing your talents will enhance all that you are. Not sharing your faith is like asking the sun not to shine, or to use the Master's illustration, 'it is like, hiding your light under a basket'. To not proclaim Christ is like someone that has perfectly healthy feet and is afraid to walk on them. The legs atrophy and become useless. Beautiful are the feet that bring good news – how beautiful are your feet?

Method and Message – Understanding the Difference

Message: Scripture, 'Gospel or good news'. The proclamation of the human condition in relation to God, in the light of both faith and faithlessness in Christ.
Method: a strategy to convey the *message*. There are several different *methods* available: a conversation travelling to a match, an evangelistic church service, a national crusade, a dinner party…

Again understanding the message of the Good News of Jesus as clearly as possible helps define and direct our strategy for sports ministry. With the *message* centrally understood we can understand the best *method* to broadcast the message. In my book *A Sporting Guide to Eternity*, I wrote, 'to dilute the Gospel *message* is to dilute its power'. We must never, change the *message*, but our approach to transmitting the *message* – the '*method*', must change and adapt with the culture. If we do not keep the method strategic our proclamation will be kept to a small group of believers, 'keeping fishbowls'. Often we seem to worship the *method* and care little for the message the *method* conveys. Seven deadly words: '*we've never done it that way before*'. In chapter 11 we will focus on several different methods for outreach. But if we don't have anything to communicate, all the slickest programmes in the world are a waste.

Formal and Informal Proclamation

There are several ways to proclaim the gospel, let's use two categories: **Formal** and **Informal**.

Formal proclamation:

Create opportunities to hear the gospel. As stated, the most effective form of proclamation is one-to-one friendship evangelism. Jesus poured his life into twelve average guys who changed the world. But Jesus did not shy away from groups large or small and He was prepared to preach when these opportunities arose. 'The large crowd listened to him with delight' (Mark 12:37). It may not be realistic for you to reach every athletic youth in your school, team or community with a one-to-one evangelistic approach. Gathering an audience is a very strategic and practical way to present the gospel. Remember a formal proclamation can be inviting your team to hear an evangelist in a stadium or gathering a couple of people around to your house to explain your faith. It is creating a window of opportunity to express your views and experiences in a more prescribed approach. Here are some of the benefits of formal proclamation:

1. **Momentum**: These 'events' work as a channel to start and drive a ministry. A big event is exciting. Getting the ball rolling is one of the toughest steps to starting a ministry.

2. **Prepared**: You can usually rally support and organise your meeting to make the presentation clear: music, speakers and multi-media. And both the presenter and the audience are primed for the message. If the audience is not aware that there will be a 'talk' they often feel manipulated and have been brought under false pretences.

3. **Create introductions:** Formal events enable you to find the people that Christ is drawing to Himself ('No one can come to me unless the Father who sent me draws him' John 6:44). Sports Outreach will rarely be involved in a big evangelistic event unless a follow-up system is in place. It is always interesting what unlikely characters God will send your way.

4. **Less personal**: Formal events are not as threatening as meeting in small groups or one-to-one. Often you can invite people to a meeting who would never darken the doors of a conventional Bible study or church service. If there is going to be a big group of people they feel they can disappear in the crowd. I often thought that Zacchaeus went up that sycamore tree (Luke 19) not only because he was short and desperate to see Jesus. I also wondered if he wanted to hide from both the crowd and the Saviour.

5. **Raise the profile**: One-off events create a visible exposure to the concept of Christianity. The exposure is effective in dispelling misconceptions (wet, weird, wally's) of Christianity. Warning – if the event is done poorly it can reinforce these conceptions. Creating a climate that is conducive to spiritual growth is key. A warm, loving welcome with genuine interest towards the guest will speak volumes but I am now digressing into the demonstration chapter.

6. **Ecumenical**: Christians are the only people I know that, when they line up for a firing squad, they gather in a circle! Sport can be one of the few ways to bring churches together.

Informal Proclamation

 We have renounced wicked and shameful ways; we do not use deception, nor do we distort the word of God. On the contrary, by setting forth the truth plainly we commend ourselves to every man's conscience in the sight of God (2 Cor. 4:2).

 You will know a man more in one hour on the games field than you will in ten hours of conversation. **Plato**

You have common ground:

Informal proclamation is using the everyday opportunities you have in the sports world to share your faith. In this compartmentalized world it is hard to build meaningful relationships, sport gives us wonderful opportunities to 'share experience'. I see many of my friends in other types of full-time ministry exhausting so much time trying to 'build relationships and find common ground' so they can earn the right to be heard. The beauty of sport is that you have a built-in source of relationship. I can talk to that guy at a party, see him at work, have lunch with him but never get the same kind of relationship I would have liked after playing nine holes of golf with him. Especially if I pay for the round!

One-to-one is scary:

Sitting in an auditorium as a young Bible student I was taken aback as Tony Campolo gave us a lesson in sociology. In a non-denominational evangelism training seminar outside of Chicago, about four thousand in attendance, Campolo asked: 'How many of you here became Christians through a Television Evangelist? About 2 per cent of the audience timidly raised their hand. Next he asked, 'how many here became Christians through a major evangelistic crusade (Big Event)'. About 10 per cent raised their hands. He then asked, 'how many became Christians through a good sermon at church?' Roughly another ten per cent raised their hands. Finally he asked, 'How many became Christians through one person being an

SPORTS OUTREACH

example and slowly encouraging and loving you into the Kingdom?' I was amazed to see the majority of people in that auditorium throw their hands into the air!

Pete Ward, former youth ministry advisor to Archbishop George Carey, has suggested throwing out all 'Big Events' in youth ministry: 'because it creates a resistance to relational ministry'. The most effective proclamation is through intimate personal relationships. One-to-one may be the most effective – but for many it is also the most scary and neglected form of proclaiming the gospel.

There will always be a gravitation towards big events (formal) ministry. Again big events are useful and create special openings and a catalyst for more concentrated ministry. Events are fun, glitzy and powerful. If you are in full-time ministry (sadly) it may help you keep your job, because events are tangibly visible. Leaders often drift to formal and away from informal proclamation because they are easy to measure: look good in front of elders and parents and give the leader kudos for bringing in someone famous. Events are easy: have a speaker, watch a film, go to a 'Crusade' or send your kids away to a camp. The widely held view of so-called 'Sports Ministry' is gathering a team around the patronage of church and maybe having a 'God Slot'. This model may assuage the conscience of the organiser but it has some way to go before it is a cohesive ministry. I have found in these types of models the athletes (whether kids or adults) are barely enduring the proclamation, and often feel manipulated. When it does not achieve the desired response they seem to blame it on the speaker. But where does the real work get done?

Conversations in the locker room: shoulder to shoulder

I thought informal evangelism meant going 'toe to toe' destroying by all means my team-mates' and friends' philosophical views, which resisted Christianity. I thought they would see the error of their ways, feel stupid in light of my theological superiority and turn to Christ. This arrogant view is successful only in alienating people, entrenching the view that Christians are 'prats'. Though defending our faith through apologetics is important, the 'toe to toe' approach is ineffective. *Ravi Zaccarias says, 'It is no good handing a man a rose after you have cut off his nose'.* The relationship built in the sports world gives us several effective opportunities to proclaim the good news of Jesus Christ 'shoulder to shoulder'. 'Be wise in the way you act toward outsiders; make the most of every opportunity. Let your conversation be always full of grace, seasoned with salt, so that you may know how to answer everyone' (Col. 4:5-6). To be honest you get little uptake in the shower about theological issues, mostly you talk about (oops women editor! better not go there!). Actually the best thing to do in a hot sticky locker room is take a shower and get changed, not have theological debates! But from the title of this paragraph everyone will understand; sport gives you fantastic opportunities for informal banter. I am the chaplain to the NFL Europe's Scottish Claymores. We were making a quick trip to Amsterdam recently to take on the Amsterdam Admirals when our flight was delayed. The objective of the players was to relieve boredom and pass time. We sat around and played cards, talked, and listened to music. It brought back so many memories of travelling with a team. The conversations start out shallow and sometimes move to insightful discussions. Whether you are enjoying road trips with a pro team or you are a soccer mom driving five-year-olds to practice, these are

SPORTS OUTREACH

priceless 'informal' opportunities for Christ. Don't be scared; don't worry about a little guff. **Ask God to give you 'opportunities', Spirit-powered guidance and a soul open for Christ**. When these windows come 'make the most' of them. Remember no one was ever forced into the Kingdom, Jesus said 'Come follow me', He never begged. You have a story – when the time is right, tell it.

A little salt:

 You have made us for yourself, and our hearts are restless until they find their rest in you. **Augustine**

 Within each of us there is a God-shaped vacuum that only God can fill.
Blaise Pascal

Have you heard the old saying you can bring a horse to water but you can't make him drink! True but you can put salt in his fodder and make him mighty thirsty. Do you remember your restless need for Christ? Recognizing your own need for God can help you convey to others **their** need for God. Perhaps you grasped that though sport was brilliant you understood that it did not satisfy the spiritual longing we all have? C.S. Lewis understood that inadequacy, and the opportunity to express it in a natural dialogue. 'I cannot offer you a watertight technique for awakening the sense of sin. I can only say that, in my experience, if one begins from the sin that has been one's own chief problem during the last week one is very often surprised at the way this shaft goes home. But whatever method we use, our continual effort must be to get their minds away from public affairs and crime and bring them down to brass tacks – to the whole network of spite, greed, envy, unfairness, and conceit in the lives of 'ordinary', decent people like themselves (and ourselves). *(Christian Reflections)*.

Lastly, listen to your team-mate. This is vital. You can never tell them where to go unless you know where they are coming from. Ask good questions and exercise all you know about listening. Perhaps if you listen to your friend they may even listen to you!

Awaking their thirst for God
When the opportunities arise here are a few questions to stimulate conversation:

- There is a system and order to this world, doesn't that suggest a system maker?
- We all agree that there are moral rules, why are we always breaking them?
  - If they don't agree, ask if molesting children is a judgement call.
- Are you interested in spiritual things?
- Since we all die, why are we afraid of it?
  - Why or why not?
  - Have you given much consideration to God?
  - Can we really know God?

- If you were God, wouldn't you want your creation to know you?
  'The heavens declare the glory of God; the skies proclaim the work of his hands' (Ps. 19:1).
- What experiences or events have shaped your views about God?
- How would you describe God?
- What do you think about Jesus?
  - How would you describe Him?
    Was He a good man?
  - How did He describe Himself?
    What relationship did He desire to have with people?
- Why is the cross a symbol known around the world?
  - What does it really mean?
  - In Romans 5 Paul wrote that God demonstrated His love for us through Christ's death, what does that mean to you?
  - How is God involved in your life?
  - What does it mean to you to be a Christian? (Listen to what your friend says, then, based on his comments, explain that a real Christian is one who has a personal relationship with Jesus Christ and trusts Him as Lord and Saviour).
  - Would you like to know God's love more personally in your life?
  - Would you like to have a better relationship with Jesus Christ?

Salt in fodder

- We are motivated when we realize that real people go to heaven and real people go to hell.
- Like any sport the more you train and the more you compete, the more proficient you become.

Note:
- During conversations your friend may come up with some off-the-wall answers, simply ask how they substantiate that? Often their explanation will nullify their reasoning.
- Often when engaged in really good conversations your friend may throw – up a 'smoke-screen'. This is usually because you are hitting a chord in their heart and the conviction is too much to bear. So consciously or unconsciously they put up barriers – topics that sidetrack you from Christ. What about homosexuals? What about all the poor people in the world? Are dogs going to heaven? Don't all religions really say the same thing? Try to bring the conversations back to Christ and the cross. Let the redeeming power of the cross do its own work.

Questions that Arise:

There is not scope in this book to produce a catalogue of apologetic answers. Here are a few examples. I do recommend that you read *Bridge Building* by Alister McGrath or *The Top 100 Questions* by Richard Bewes.

Who made God?

Answer: If God was made He would not be the supreme being. If some other god made God it would not make sense. Follow it out: who made God? A super god made God? Who made the super god? A super, super god. Who made the super, super god? A super, super... God is the supreme being. We have a finite mind so it is difficult to completely grasp an infinite God. That is why God sent His son in the form of a man...

Aren't there several ways to heaven?

Answer: I agree with you that there are several claims to getting to heaven. But Jesus was exclusive. John 14:6: 'Jesus answered, 'I am the way and the truth and the life. No one comes to the Father except through me.' C S Lewis said, 'Either Jesus was a liar and he was not the Messiah, or he was a lunatic or he was who he said he was the Lord.' There is no middle ground with Jesus. Jesus also said that the way to heaven was very narrow, he did not give a soft-sell answer.

How can there be a good God when bad things happen in the world?

Answer: This is difficult to answer from our prospective. But first show me where it says in the Scriptures that everything will be easy. From the beginning of the third chapter of Genesis we see that man's disobedience brought sin into the world. Sin breaks everything, even nature. God has given us a plan and a Saviour to fix sin. But we were given a free will. We can either reject our Creator or humble ourselves and give glory to our Creator. The abuse of free will is dangerous; we do indeed live in a dangerous world.

Isn't the Bible full of mistakes, like a Chinese whisper?

Long answer: In 1947 an Arab shepherd boy herding his sheep found the archaeologist's dream! The boy wandered into an ancient burial ground of a large quasi-Jewish community; a community that meticulously preserved ancient manuscripts and scripture (the dead sea scrolls). The oldest copy we have of the book of Isaiah was found and the significance is that through hundreds of years the transmission the Scriptures did not change. Scribes that copied the Bible were painstakingly accurate.

Short answer: Isn't it great that the main points of Scripture are repeated over and over!

SPORTS OUTREACH

 # The Cringe Factor

But we preach Christ crucified: a stumbling block to Jews and foolishness to gentiles (1 Cor. 1:24).

If someone asks me one more time to give a non-cringy address at their evangelistic event I am going to slap them! Okay so maybe I won't slap them, I agree I certainly do not want to be insincere, insensitive, overbearing, irrelevant and especially not arrogant in my presentation. I am all against manipulation and forcing Christianity down peoples' throats (I weigh 18 ½ stone – if ramming Christ down throats worked I'd do it). But tell me, how does one hear a clear communication of the gospel and not cringe! The message of the cross is strong, effectual and, to a seeker, often confusing (there is a war being waged in their soul). The Gospel is gut-wrenching. I have to compliment men all over the world – we have done an incredible job! We've taken the most amazing story: Christ's birth, life, teachings, miracles, death and resurrection, the most startling story in the world, and we've made it boring and inoffensive. That takes enterprise. Tell me how you can sit at Christ's feet as He hung to the cross and not wince knowing that you put Him there?

Presenting the gospel is clearly expensive. It may cost you your worldly dignity.

You may appear the 'fool' to your team-mates. But whether you are sharing your faith to one team-mate or to the whole league, the power comes from 'preaching Christ and Christ crucified'. The benefits of being a Christian: new faith, freedom from guilt, hope… are brilliant, but the life-changing power comes from what Christ did for us on the cross. Beating around the bush just muddles the message. Perhaps cringing at the truth is better than cringing later without it.

CHAPTER SIX
DEMONSTRATION

VISUALISATION OF TRUTH

Question: *'Teacher, which is the greatest commandment in the Law?'*
Answer: *Jesus replied: '"Love the Lord your God with all your heart and all your soul and with all your mind." This is the first and greatest commandment. And the second is like it: "Love your neighbour as yourself." All the law and the prophets hang on these two commandments.'*
Question: *'And who is my neighbour?'*
Answer: *The expert of the law replied, 'The one who had mercy on him.'*
Action: *Jesus told him, 'Go and do likewise.'*

Your talk talks and your walk talks, but your walk talks louder than your talk talks.
Fellowship of Christian Athletes

The best way to teach a concept is by modelling it. **Harvard Business School**

But God demonstrates his own love for us in this: While were still sinners, Christ died for us **(Rom. 5:8).**

SPORTS OUTREACH

THE Word of God is powerful but it can be made impotent if it is not linked to an actual demonstration of God's love 'incarnate' in us. Young people will see right through another student that is a two-faced hypocrite. They say one thing but their actions are far from living the truth. Today the best advertisement for Christianity is Christians. Jesus' method for transmitting the 'Good News' was people. I remember the retired pro-American football player seething during a 'kiss and tell' style television interview as he described how: 'My Coach... was too busy to even bother visiting me in the hospital after my career ending injury! And he... calls himself a Christian!' I certainly do not know the whole story but I know the coach and respect him. But I wonder what a trip to the hospital could have done to help open that player's heart to the gospel. In Jesus' narrative of the Good Samaritan we always despise the two religious chaps who, on seeing the man who was beat up by robbers 'passed by on the other side' (Luke 10:33). They missed a super opportunity to glorify God. How many times have we done the same?

 Scenario:

For a week you are pestered by your friend to come to 'sports-day' – a basketball tournament being held next Saturday. Your pal vaguely mentions that a 'church has organised it, but it will be cool'. You feel a little nervous showing up to a church-function; you hadn't been remotely involved with a church since your uncle Robert got married, again! But you agree to go since it will be held at a neighbouring rec.-centre. The atmosphere seems strange and you feel a little ignored by other kids you have seen in school; some of the kids seem to be surprised that you are there. Finally, as you are herded into teams by a couple of guys that don't really seem to know what is going on, your pal shows up. You try to find out what the day is all about and again your buddy does not seem to know. At last you are playing in a tournament but it is immediately obvious that the play is second-rate and the referees are 'clearly clueless'. One of your opponents (in your mind you call him, 'Mr Flash'), is an old looking guy of about twenty-six. He is still a pretty good ball handler, but you get the impression that he is only there to show-off. Sadly every move he makes says, 'hey look at me – I'm still cool'. The same guy fouls you but when you protest the ref. acts like you are a jerk and says, 'hey man it's only a game, no big deal'. 'No big deal' – sport is your life and these idiots don't seem to care about the integrity of the game!

Finally, the tournament is over, you feel a bit awkward with your cheap third-place pin that says 'We are all winners in Jesus'. Another old guy with flash clothes who seems to be trying to act like a pop star says, 'we are going to sing a few songs'. So you are herded over into a corner of the gym and he starts singing. You don't recognise a single song, which compounds your embarrassment because you seem to be the only one in this parallel universe that doesn't. Then the 'flash guy' that has acted like he was the next Michael Jordon (after all he is wearing all his clothes – the same kit you wish you could afford) stands up to speak. He shows off his first place pin and acts like he won the NBA. You are surprised he is representing the church, you think to yourself that he is a pretty bad advertisement for religion. Then Mr Flash starts speaking and he uses some indistinguishable religious words which sound like they came from a Shakespeare play. Slowly it dawns on you that he is preaching, and it seems to be focused at you. Inside you start to smoulder as you realise you were brought under false pretences. You cannot wait to get out of the room and you say to yourself that if that is Christianity you want nothing to do with it.

This is an exaggerated illustration to make a point; **proclamation** without **demonstration** is dangerous to the Great Commission. Being genuine, sincere and authentic are the qualities of demonstration. To adhere to Jesus' message is to put your life into radical demonstration of Jesus' teachings. We are commanded to love our neighbour. *'And the second is like it: "Love your neighbour as yourself." All the law and the prophets hang on these two commandments.'* Let me ask you, is the word love used as a noun or a verb? It is a verb – it denotes action.

Much of my time in Scotland is spent with professional sports people. Eating dinner with two Christians that play football in the Scottish Premier League recently I heard the highest praise one player could brag about the other. 'He is the best example for Christ. He is always on time, always organised and usually has a smile on his face, even the morning after a big defeat. Our team knows he is a Christian and they can see it!'

Any Fruit Under those Leaves?

When God's nature is possessed, His purposes are presented. In a recent Bible study with some professional American Footballers we were studying Matthew 7: 'By their fruit you will recognize them. Do people pick grapes from thorn bushes, or figs from thistles? Likewise every good tree bears good fruit, but a bad tree bears bad fruit.' I mentioned that in sport you couldn't hide for long. The truth of your character is revealed due to the nature of sport; you are exposed. You are in a world of heightened emotion and your team-mates and coaches will know you by your actions (fruit) pretty fast. A defensive back in the study admitted he had to watch his mouth. He loved to 'trash talk', and started to realise that his language did not match his new-found faith in Christ. He went on to tell a story that reinforced to all of us the importance of bringing our actions in line with faith.

 I had always been a 'trash talker', thinking somehow that it gave me an edge on the field. That is until I was playing against the University of Texas. I

admired Texas's running back as a great player and an out-spoken Christian. I was a young Christian with a lot of bad habits. To be honest my team-mates laughed at my faith, mainly because I was so inconsistent. In the game against Texas, I made a superb tackle (I don't mind saying) against this Christian running back. I nailed him! One of those tackles when you hear seventy-thousand people go – ooohhh! I popped up and got in his face so bad, telling him he was nothing and words we definitely don't use in bible study. I thought this would psyche him out! But do you know what he did! He popped up and replied to me with the most sincere grin, 'Hey 26 (my number) that was a good tackle, God bless you, I'm going to pray for you'. I could not believe it; he shut me up in a New York second! I went back to the huddle with more admiration for him and shame of myself. I learned a great lesson in following Jesus that day!

What do you Smell Like?

When we came to Britain over a decade ago, to help develop sports ministry and also coach the Oxford American football team, my wife and I heard that the British liked tea. Michelle and I were not tea drinkers (things have changed), we had little exposure to tea and if we drank any, it was herbal tea. Herbal tea in the UK (for my American readers), especially in the early nineties, was taken as a natural medicine, less for general consumption. So when my assistant coach Steve Abbott, our first guest, arrived on our doorstep to welcome us, we sat him down on rugby dummies (since our furniture had not yet arrived) and offered him a drink. He asked for tea and received a lesson in cross-cultural differences. Soon we were enjoying talking American football strategy for the upcoming season; my wife, always the hostess, came into the living room with her first offering of tea in our new country. She handed it to my assistant coach who accepted it gratefully, and we were soon engrossed in our playbook. Slowly I began to notice, to my embarrassment and amusement, his desperate attempt to disguise his displeasure in drinking the revolting liquid. True to form he was courteous and never communicated his dissatisfaction (a skill I wished all assistant coaches would learn). After a couple of hours he gradually emptied the mug. Neither my wife nor I liked tea so we understood the taste was unappealing, but what we did not understand was how bad this tea tasted! The next day I was teasing Steve when he finally admitted in the locker-room, away from my wife, that our tea was 'nasty'. When he found out it was herbal tea (with milk) he laughed and laughed, explaining he, 'never drank herbal tea especially with milk and sugar!'

We soon sought counsel from a neighbour who was the local farmer's wife. She taught us to make a 'proper cup of tea'. We went through the whole procedure including: heating the porcelain teapot with water, pouring out the water and putting in more boiling water; then pouring in loose-leaf tea; next, waiting for the tea to brew, then, using a tea strainer, pouring the tea into the cups.

What is interesting about the procedure is that the hot water takes on the colour, aroma and flavour of tea. Incarnation is about the Holy Spirit entering us and we take on the aroma, colour and flavour of Christ. 'But thanks be to God, who always leads us in triumphal procession in Christ and through us spreads everywhere the fragrance of the knowledge of him.' Christ rested His ministry on those that so loved Him and who were so passionate about Him that their lives emanated Christ.

Of all the teams I played for, my warmest memories come from my high school. Our coach Jim Rexilius (Coach Rex) is a legend and there was no doubt whose team we were playing for. If a coach saw a couple of kids go to university from his high school to compete he would feel good about his school's sports programme; our school to date has had fifteen kids become professional American footballers. Our team took on the characteristics of our coach. Coach Rex was disciplined, intense and brutally fair – even his own children had to prove themselves (which they did) twice as worthy before he would play them. Our team was conditioned (the best conditioned I have ever been) and had little flair. We were drilled in the fundamentals and executed our technique well under pressure. We had mental toughness and very little patience for screw-ups. We loved each other (for the most part) and have stayed in contact more so than any other team I have played for. In essence we took on the characteristics of the coach. Our team embodied his spirit. My coach is a Christian and many of the qualities of the coach we embodied were characteristics of Christ.

We Gravitate to our Strengths

I encounter many dads training their children to play football/soccer in their back gardens, the good ones will insist their child passes the ball equally with their less dominant foot. I heard of one dad putting a slipper on his son's right foot so he would learn to kick left-footed. This is an illustration you see often in sport. Athletes play to their strengths but will rarely develop their weaknesses. A great athlete will stretch himself and develop a well-rounded game. The rest rely on only what they are good at and when they try for the big leagues, they fall away. Attentiveness to balance is key.

Some readers will immediately gravitate to the **Proclamation** and others will be pulled towards **Demonstration**. But balance is vital. Some will be very good with words and others are better with actions, but to be balanced is most effective. I would like to sew the lips shut of some evangelists and tell them to go win someone to the Lord with their actions. They blab, blab, blab about showing God's love, they enjoy talking strategy for outreach, and they wax eloquent about the majesty of our Lord. But if you are in a jam and ask them to help you move a battered wife, loan you their house or help paint the office, they are never around. In contrast, some Christians always show up for the service ministries with warm happy smiles. Ask them to move chairs, serve coffee, clean toilets and pick up kids all over the city and they are there! When it comes to demonstrating God's love in a happy generous way they are great; that's their deal. They are servers and happy to do it. Ask the demonstrator to share their faith, and you run into a stone wall. The 'para-bible' excuses come flying: it is not my gift, I do not want to turn them off, I need to get to know them better...

SPORTS OUTREACH

We gravitate to our strengths at the peril of our weaknesses. Now I know that there are different parts of the body and our Lord has given us all unique gifts to use for His Kingdom. Athletic teams come in all shapes, talents and sizes; so does the 'body' of the church. But Jesus also encouraged us to maximise our talents and other talents will be added for His purposes and His glory.

 ## Do you do the Dishes?

Regardless of the unique gifts of the body of Christ, none of us is exempt from *Proclaiming* the gospel. Neither are any of us exempt from *Demonstrating* the gospel. One thing stands out about the gifted evangelist Billy Graham who has preached the gospel to more people than any one else in the world. Graham did the washing-up! Billy Graham was humble. No attitude. I remember as a university student visiting a neighbouring university to see a buddy. We were studying in the library when suddenly several of the students started staring at a group of 'quite dignified' and important looking people. There was a bit of a swagger to the group, a couple of them were wearing cowboy hats, in Chicago! One guy walked by and put his hand on my shoulder gave me a warm grin and nodded. I thought what a nice old dude, my next thought was that I had seen that guy somewhere. Later that day I realised Billy Graham was in town and he was the very guy that had nodded to me. I have never met Graham again but of course admired him from afar. I read about or occasionally work with guys that knew him well, strangely they always mention to me with surprise, 'Did you know Graham was always quick to do the dishes?' I am not surprised. Graham always shunned the pretence of superstardom. Demonstration of the gospel is powerful.

The Apostle Paul loved to make lists. He gives us a string of qualities to remember in every letter he wrote. In the book of Titus we find Paul encouraging the young Christian leader he is writing to. He is on Crete, an island in the Mediterranean Sea. The morals of the island had sunk shamefully low, and dishonesty, gluttony and laziness were what the island had become famous for. They needed someone to be an example and Paul, ever the Christian entrepreneur, recruits Titus for the job. In the book of Titus we find Paul bolstering his young protégé with these encouraging words: 'In everything, set them an example by doing what is good. In your teaching show integrity, seriousness and soundness of speech that cannot be condemned so that those who oppose you may be ashamed because they have nothing bad to say about us' (Titus 2:6). Later Paul again urges Titus to 'stress these things, so that those who have trusted in God may be careful to devote themselves to doing what is good' (Titus 3:8). Paul, like a sports coach, keeps pounding into his apprentice a most important principle: 'demonstrate God in your life: do what is good.' Our faith is not just for Sunday, walk the walk.

Influence

'There are little eyes upon you,
And they're watching night and day;
There are little ears that quickly
Take in every word you say;
There are little hands all eager
To do anything you do;
And a little boy who's dreaming
of the day he'll be like you.

You're the little fellow's idol;
You're the wisest of the wise,
In his little mind about you,
No suspicions ever rise;
He believes in you devoutly,
Holds that all you say and do,
He will say and do, in your way
When he's a grown-up like you.
There's a wide-eyed little fellow,
Who believes you are always right,
And his ears are always open,
And he watches day and night;
You are setting an example
Every day in all you do,
For the little boy who's waiting
To grow up to be like you."

Author unknown

CHAPTER SEVEN
MATURATION

CULTIVATION OF TRUTH

 Nourish: to provide all that is necessary for growth.

 To prepare God's people for works of service, so that the body of Christ may be built up until we all reach unity in the faith and in the knowledge of the Son of God and become <u>mature</u>, attaining to the whole measure of the fullness of Christ (**Eph. 4:12**).

Incubation + Education + Application = Maturation

NOBODY would expect me to be a scratch golfer after my second golf lesson. I am surprised when people take up a sport and expect to be a pro over night. I remember dragging myself out onto Huntington Beach day after day (I think I should have been studying) until finally, after weeks of failure, I was able to get up for a few seconds on my surfboard. It looked so easy from the beach. Becoming spiritually mature looks easy. You collect a new vocabulary; you learn to smile at the right time. You carry a Bible and whamo you are St Augustine. Not exactly. Growing in Christ and helping others to grow is a lifelong ministry

SPORTS OUTREACH

– it takes a concerted effort, goals and coaching. Rick Warren writes in *The Purpose Driven Church*, 'Maturity Myth #1: Spiritual growth is automatic once you are born again: Many churches have no organized plan for following up on new believers and no comprehensive strategy for developing members to maturity. They leave it all to chance, assuming that Christians will automatically grow in maturity if they attend church services.'

As I meet with church group after group that is interested in sports ministry I am disheartened by the fact that all they want to do are proclamation events. In other words, they want a famous sports star to come to their church and speak. That is it: no strategic plan on bringing the few God may draw to Him to maturity in Him. Robert Coleman speaking of Jesus' formal proclamation, in *Master Plan of Evangelism* writes, 'What good would it have been for his ultimate objective to arouse the masses to follow him if these people had no subsequent supervision or instruction in the Way?' Our third principle is not glamorous, it is not high profile, you receive little recognition for doing it. **But setting up a system for growing Christians is key and should be implemented from the beginning of your sports ministry.** A favourite subject for Christ was 'seeds'. 'Though it is the smallest of all your seeds, yet when it grows...', 'But if it dies, it produces many seeds...', 'But the seed on good soil stands for those with a noble and good heart, who hear the word, retain it, and by persevering produce a crop.' What do seeds do? They grow and produce. We are called as sports ministers to grow and produce a crop of sports people that love and want to serve Christ.

Incubation: Climate and Time for Spiritual Growth

Live purposefully and worthily and accurately, making the very most of the time, buying up each opportunity, because the days are evil (**Eph. 5:15-16** AMP. v).

 Scenario:

Imagine the scene: a premature baby is delivered in the hospital. She comes out of the warm gentle climate of her mother's womb into the harsh world. But fortunately there is an incubator ready for her and she is given the oxygen and care that she needs to survive. After an hour a loud masculine looking female nurse comes in and says 'time to go home, luv', wishes them good luck, and throws the mother and baby out into the street with a donation envelope for the incubator fund!

This sounds like an unlikely scenario, but do we do the same with new Christians? We are overjoyed when we see them put their hand up at an appeal, but from then on we expect them to live perfect Christian lives as if they have always been in the church. We need to create a climate that is conducive to spiritual growth and then give it as much time as possible. A climate of a clear *proclamation* of the gospel that is *demonstrated* in real practical actions is the perfect place to **grow** spiritually. Time is the next key factor in ministry. **You do not get quality disciples without quantities of time.** It is like cracking the chrysalis of a cocoon an hour after it is formed and expecting to find a beautiful butterfly. No matter how wonderfully the cocoon is formed, maturity has to take place. I remember a young youth minister speaking at a conference saying, 'I am in youth ministry for the long haul with a three-year contract!' A seasoned youth minister was next to speak and mentioned, 'when I was twenty-three three years seemed like the 'long haul' to me as well'.

You can have the greatest climate in the world but time is imperative. We have too many premature Christian babies struggling in this world. Many of these mistakes can be corrected with forward planning and faith that God will actually move in the lives of the people you are called to work with. Many of you, even while reading this, may never have had a mentoring relationship. You may have been thrust out into the world with little to equip you, and I am not talking about a degree in theology. Miraculously you stumbled onto some good soil and in spite of the climate grew into a strong Christian. Let me challenge you to take up a new skill – mentoring. You will have to learn to mentor while never having been mentored yourself. Before His disciples, Christ performed miracles, was crucified and resurrected. But we seem to overlook that He also shared in the most common life experiences. These day-to-day experiences created opportunities for spiritual growth. Jesus followers gathered around Christ and watched Him live; time with Jesus created a healthy climate, an incubator. Let us look at Christ's example and try to extract some discipleship principles.

He lived with them:
- 'Leaving Nazareth, he went and lived in Capernaum' (Matt. 4:13).

He recruited them:
- '"Follow me", he told him, and Matthew got up and followed him' (Matt. 9:9).

He challenged them:
- 'I will make you fishers of men' (Matt. 4:19).

He encouraged them:
- 'Then Jesus told his disciples a parable to show them that they should always pray and not give up' (Luke 18:1).

He socialised with them:
- 'Jesus and his disciples had also been invited to the wedding in Cana' (John 2:2).

SPORTS OUTREACH

He ate with them:
- 'While Jesus was having dinner at Matthew's house, many tax collectors and 'sinners' came and ate with him and his disciples' (Matt. 9:10).

He travelled with them:
- 'After this, Jesus travelled about from one town and village to another, proclaiming the good news of the kingdom of God. The Twelve were with him' (Luke 8:1).

He talked to them:
- 'Were not our hearts burning within us while he talked with us on the road and opened the Scriptures to us?' (Luke 24:32).

He taught them:
- 'This, then, is how you should pray:' (Matt. 6:9).

He corrected them:
- 'Jesus turned and said to Peter, "Get behind me, Satan! You are a stumbling block to me; you do not have in mind the things of God, but the things of men"' (Matt. 16:23).

He celebrated with them:
- 'He replied, "Go into the city to a certain man and tell him, The Teacher says: My appointed time is near. I am going to celebrate the Passover with my disciples at your house"' (Matt. 26:18).

*adapted from the FCA Training Manual

Jesus spent casual time with the people He discipled. It was not a mentoring programme, it was a mentoring life. You cannot do it with a big group, it has to be small and intimate. It is not a formal programme, though you will teach the Bible, it is more personal. And it can last a long time. I mentioned my high school coach in the previous chapter, Coach Rex. He is in his seventies now, and I am in my forties. He still encourages me, and he still takes an interest in my spiritual walk with God. 'Connor stay on your knees.' What an example that is to me of long-term discipleship. There are times that I feel spiritually weak, in those times I draw on a special strength from guys that have been in the game a lot longer than me.

 Recruiting

You never see Jesus begging His disciples to follow Him. He never backed down on His requirements. Take the rich young ruler as an example.

'Now a man came up to Jesus and asked, "Teacher, what good thing must I do to get eternal life?" "Why do you ask me about what is good?" Jesus replied.

"There is only One who is good. If you want to enter life, obey the commandments." "Which ones?" the man inquired. Jesus replied, "Do not murder, do not commit adultery, do not steal, do not give false testimony, honor your father and mother, and love your neighbor as yourself." "All these I have kept," the young man said. "What do I still lack?" Jesus answered, "If you want to be perfect, go, sell your possessions and give to the poor, and you will have treasure in heaven. Then come, follow me." When the young man heard this, he went away sad, because he had great wealth' (Matt. 19:17-22).

The Rich Young Man looks to us like a fantastic recruit. He had means that could have helped Christ in His social programs; he was young so there would have been a big future in his ministry. He was moral, Jesus would not have worried about a scandal of His disciples hurting the cause with a rogue that got a girl pregnant or ran off with the ministry donations. He was also a leader, able to challenge, organise and strategise future outreaches and campaigns. This guy appeared to be the perfect candidate for leadership training. But he was greedy. Jesus saw the trouble he would be and gave him a tough assignment – go sell all you have and give it to the poor. It is not remarkable that this guy left, what is remarkable is that Jesus did not run after him! We never see Jesus saying, 'Oh please, please stay I really didn't mean it. You are a good guy and maybe you can give a tenth away when you feel like it.' Jesus let him go and spent time with the candidates that were open. Remarkably.

If we look at many of the leaders in the Bible, we see that a lot more time went into their training and preparation than we might realise at first.

- Moses was 80 before God chose him to lead the Israelites out of Egypt, and God thought that they needed 40 years to learn the lessons He had for them before they entered Canaan.
- Jesus spent thirty years preparing for His ministry. He spent an intensive three years with His disciples before His death and resurrection.
- Paul spent three years in Arabia learning from God before he commenced his ministry (Gal. 1:18).

Ministry is a marathon:
Whenever the Apostle Paul describes the Christian life he seems to be implying a marathon, not a one hundred meter dash. There is a different mental preparation required for a marathon than a sprint. A marathon requires endurance, perseverance and encouragement to keep going. We need to view discipleship as a marathon instead of a sprint. Ministry is more than a ten second cheer from the stands as our people dash by. We run alongside them, offer them water, encourage them, run the hills with them, see them through to the

SPORTS OUTREACH

end, or at least as far as we can run together. Imagine that heaven is like the end of a long distance race and you are watching to see your discipleship group come in – 'where is Alex, Oh there he is, he's nearly there, where's Susan – she's struggling, I'll run down and help her up the hill...' We need to have a vision for seeing people through to the end of the race, rather than setting them on their way and wishing them all the best. So how do we practically help people over the long haul?

Education: Direction and Tools for Spiritual Maturity

 If you hold to my teaching, you are really my disciples. Then you will know the truth, and the truth will set you free (John 8:31-32).

Ideas into action:

This section is education, but we must be careful by the connotation, I do not mean the mere acquisition of Bible facts. Head knowledge is not heart knowledge. Pastor James MacDonald of Harvest Church near Chicago calls people who live solely to learn Bible facts as 'Bible-Fatheads', 'they go from one conference to another acquiring more and more information, yet never utilising the information.' Bible-Fatheads feel that the mere memorisation of information is a sacrament. The victorious Christian life does not mean winning 'Bible Trivia'. There is no maturation from the mere accumulation of information. In fact Paul may be alluding to the dangers of becoming arrogant by simply possessing facts: **'*knowledge puffs up, but love builds up*'** (1 Cor. 8:1).

Our education must convey a sense of immediacy; an action will be required from the information received. The goal of maturation is not to know more *about Christ* but to become more *like Christ*. Our teaching has purpose when we understand that our education is meant to protect, train and equip us for a lifetime of building God's Kingdom through spiritual battle.

 I have hidden your word in my heart that I might not sin against you (Ps. 119:11).

Education protects:

When we understand that we are in spiritual battle we will want to protect our flock. Teaching biblical principles and equipping your flock to access these truths and promises for themselves is key. Acquiring a foundation of biblical principles and having a working understanding of theology is paramount. I cannot emphasise this enough, God speaks directly from the pages of His book. In many churches and sports ministry organisations there seems to be less importance on finding a leader with biblical qualifications than there is on athletic qualifications. Our aim in education is to prepare. Paul stresses to his young apprentice Timothy to: teach, train and equip. *'But as for you, continue in what you have learned and become convinced of, because you know those from whom you learned it, and how from infancy you have known the holy Scriptures, which are able to make you wise for salvation through faith in Christ Jesus. All scripture is God-breathed and is useful for teaching, rebuking, correcting and training in righteousness, so that the man of God may be thoroughly equipped for every good work.'* Vision-casting for young or stagnant Christians is vital. Quite often after making a decision for Christ, a young Christian feels they have arrived. Being a 'serious Christian', one that prays, asks for forgiveness, gives away their money and/or shares their faith, seems to be an option. When a young Christian is exposed to immature Christians (Christians who should be stronger in their faith), this only confirms the 'option scheme'. 'I will take a bit of this righteousness, or a touch of that forgiveness, a lot of that blessing, after all Righteous Raymond does not seem to be bothered with the poor, so why should I.' Expressing the lifelong journey of discipleship is essential to a healthy Christian life. Explaining the purpose of every Christian, challenging the Christian to explore the precepts and promises that they were given in Scripture, will give them tools for life.

Teach the Bible:

Sadly some people in ministry are intimidated by the Bible and rely on the ***demonstration*** of God's word but not ***proclaiming*** His Word. Your shortcomings usually infect your ministry. If you are biblically anaemic your disciples become biblically anaemic. To be Christian leaders we need to be lifelong students of His Word. Again, to encourage spirituality we need to model maturity. Often leaders in sports ministry will tell me they are too busy to get into their Bibles, their sport is too demanding. I tell them then what you are saying, that in your life sport is number one and God is number two. You have no business leading a group! But if I don't lead it who will? This will be covered further in the next chapter, 'Building Leaders'. But if I could encourage you that in twenty years of ministry the best ministers in the world of sport are not scholars. But they are committed to understanding better the Word of God and teaching it to others. Anyone who does not value biblical teaching should not be doing ministry.

Practical teaching:

Teach with **Conviction**. Aren't you glad God gave us a book! Teach it as God's very word.

Teach with **Inspiration**. Inspire comes from 'In-Spirit', God promised you the gift of the Holy Spirit to help guide and encourage.

Teach with **Clarity**. A W Tozer said about preaching, 'Get the ideas understood and the words will come.' Do not try to muddle through a passage you do not understand. Get help to clarify the point before you try to convey it.

Teach in **Context**. Work hard to understand what the whole passage is saying. What precedes and follows the verses you are working on will connect. Taking a passage out of context is dangerous.

Teach in **Humility.** Questions will arise which you cannot answer. Don't worry, you are in good company. Admit you do not know the answer, but you will try to find out the answer or someone who can answer.

Teach in **Love.** When we are motivated by love, our teaching of Scriptures becomes animated and winsome. The characters, principles and precepts come to life.

ASK YOURSELF:
- Am I learning new insights from Scripture?
- Am I giving my best in preparation or just winging it?
- Have I gone to a conference lately?
- Am I rehashing the same old lessons?
- Am I intimidated when a more knowledgeable Bible teacher is in the room while I am giving a lesson?

SPORTS OUTREACH

Application: Ideas into Actions

 I pray that you may be active in sharing your faith, so that you will have a full understanding of every good thing we have in Christ (**Philem. 6**).

Norm Evans is the director of the Pro Athletes Outreach (PAO). Much of the ministry he and his wife Bobbe do, is equipping pros to be strong Christians in the strange world of professional sports. A major component of their ministry is 'Training Conferences'. These pros are taken away from their hectic schedules to be taught, encouraged and equipped. The conferences' settings, facilities and food are always first-class. They provide brilliant speakers who are not afraid to stand in front of national heroes and give a clear proclamation of the Gospel. PAO conferences also provide seminars that give life skills to the unique challenge and privileges that professional athletes encounter. Often the seminars include, How to read your Bible, How to manage your financial resources, How to pray, Christian family values and How to share your faith. I remember helping run one of those seminars on 'Sharing your faith'. The guys in attendance were good guys who have been coached all their lives. These 'pros' understood discipline and teamwork; athletes are generally good at assimilating facts into action. But when you are in seminar after seminar even the best teaching gets monotonous. Norm understands this and always incorporates a 'Field-Trip' midway into the conference.

Ask him about the 'Field-Trip' and he will give you a wry, almost sadistic grin. Like a coach getting his team in shape, Norm knows these field trips are a fundamental element of the conference. You may think a PAO 'Field-Trip' is a break in the conference to visit a beautiful beach or go shopping in an expensive mall. Quite the opposite, the 'Field-Trips' are usually to an orphanage or juvenile penitentiary where the athletes have an opportunity to present the gospel. While some of the pros can't wait to get on the bus many are apprehensive having never shared their faith before and some even feign sickness (they are probably sick with nerves!). It may seem strange that though these pros can compete seemingly undaunted before thousands in a stadium, and millions on television would be frightened standing in front of thirty kids at an orphanage. But they are and it is our job to pile them onto the bus. I remember Norman say to me, 'if you want to build leaders you have to sometimes, let them fail'.

We pile off the bus and warily these giant good-looking guys edge into the chapel. You can see them try to remember the academic lessons they learned in their previous seminars. It is funny to see guys try to hide behind each other hoping Evans will not call on them, they are more nervous than playing in a championship. I remember one guy after getting picked trying to express his faith, he wavered one foot to another, looking back at his friends for support, and then thought he had a line, 'Remember Christianity is Aahhh – Aahhh – kinda like Aahhh. Aahhh – kinda like Christmas! – You know – you gotta be good!' You can see Norm and the rest of the seminar leaders roll their heads back in frustration mixed with amusement. Norm jumps in and gives a clear presentation of the gospel, including grace (unmerited favour on God's part), and we quietly go back to the hotel, shaking our heads. But that night, back in the seminars the professionals are taking notes like their lives depended on it! They tasted Kingdom-building and they want more. The teaching is not theory anymore, it's winning souls for Christ. They have seen these kids close-up and they experienced first-hand the excitement and difficulty in presenting Christ. They better understand the joy and their own particular deficiencies. They are motivated to learn. Why – because there was a direct application!

How many people are in ministry today because someone gave them a challenge to share their testimony! 'But you are a chosen people, a royal priesthood, a holy nation, a people belonging to God, that you may declare the praises of him who called you out of darkness into his wonderful light' (1 Pet. 2:9). Anyone in full-time ministry should be creating opportunities for others to do ministry. There is also a mothering approach that is suffocating. We need to send them out and experience the work. If we never give our disciples opportunities to serve how can they apply what they are learning? I remember preaching at a certain denominational conference on 'impacting your world for Christ'. One attendee admitted jokingly, we are never encouraged to apply what we learn we are only asked to, 'pay and pray'. I truly believe in the priesthood of all believers – that we should all be doing ministry. Elton Trueblood said, 'A non-ministering Christian is a contradiction in terms.' Scriptures were given to live by not merely memorise. The job of anyone in leadership is to create opportunities for ministry for all to minister. A leader's job is to hand out fishing-rods so we can all fish. More on this in our next chapter on reproducing.

The sooner we mobilise our group the better. When we see a faith community with many of the members mobilised in ministry we say, '*extraordinary*', but in terms of New Testament theology we must confess it should be *the norm*!

Practical Concerns:

Application of course means more than just vocalising your faith, it may mean encouraging your flock to pray regularly, give away resources and exercise any number of talents. Application is using the unique gifts and abilities given to you and those you have been charged with and using them to glorify our Creator. *'For we are God's workmanship, created in Christ Jesus to do good works, which God prepared in advance for us to do' (Eph. 2:10).* The danger occurs when the leader never challenges their flock to grow up. In the same way the mother who always picks up her son's socks is never going to teach him to tidy up.

There is always a fine line creating opportunities for young Christians to share their faith. It is risky and can be dangerous if not controlled by mature Christians. But the benefit is a multiplication of ministry not just addition.

Ask yourself:

- Do I provide opportunities for ministry?
- Do I just teach principles or do I give concrete application to my teaching?
- What are my motives for being in the spotlight?
- Am I encouraging others to use their gifts or merely wanting them to be impressed with mine?
- Could I give up my pulpit occasionally to allow for my young members to gain experience teaching?
- Do I value other forms of ministry?
    - Is my ministry a good climate for spiritual growth?
    - Am I mentoring others or merely following a programme?
    - Do I spend meaningful time with my group?
    - Do I socialise with my group?
    - Have I called an old disciple and asked them how they were doing lately?

Maturity is not a quick fix programme but a long-term journey, a journey to experience and to encourage. So grow strong and in the next chapter we will look closer at how to grow a whole army of sports ministers.

CHAPTER EIGHT
REPRODUCTION

REPRODUCING REPRODUCERS

And the things you have heard me say in the presence of many witnesses, entrust to reliable men who will also be qualified to teach others **(2 Tim. 2:2).**

What reliable men and women have I poured my life into?

Begin with the Beginning in Mind!

Suppose one of you wants to build a tower. Will he not first sit down and estimate the cost to see if he has enough money to complete it? For if he lays the foundation and is not able to finish it, everyone who sees it will ridicule him, saying, "This fellow began to build and was not able to finish" **(Luke 14:30).**

SPORTS OUTREACH

IN sport for the most part you have clear objectives: guidelines, sidelines and finish lines. Stephen Covey's now classic motivational book, *The Seven Habits of Highly Effective People*, helps you identify and focus on clear objectives in the secular world. In the books, *Second Habit* and *Begin with the End in Mind*, the reader is encouraged to 'start with a clear understanding of your destination'. 'To begin with the end in mind' is based on the principle that all things are created twice. There's a mental creation, and a physical creation to all things'. 'To begin with the end in mind means to start with a clear understanding of your objective'. Dr Covey cloaks many biblical principles into an easy-reading business leadership format. I am not surprised to read that the book has sold over ten million copies, or that he has given guidance to many. But there is another reason he has been so successful, he does not give you the complete truth. If he did, the book would never have been published. He stops short of every human's ultimate journey, standing before God at the judgement seat, – he does not give his readers the true 'end in mind': heaven or hell! 'Therefore God exalted him to the highest place and gave him the name that is above every name, that at the name of Jesus every knee should bow, in heaven and on earth and under the earth...' (Phil. 2:10).

We certainly all do have a destiny, and understanding that destiny will better focus our objectives. So plan your objectives around your beginning! Your eternal life with Christ! 'But for them it was only the beginning of the real story. All their life in Narnia had only been the cover and the title page: now at last they were beginning Chapter One of the Great Story which no one on earth has read: which goes on forever: in which every chapter is better than the one before' (C S Lewis *The Last Battle*).

The professional golfer Paul Azinger got the message one-third of the world will hear, 'you have a life-threatening form of cancer'. These kinds of messages open up a hard window on reality and our priorities are quickly realigned. Many things we greatly value seem to lose their worth, other things become priceless. All Azinger could think of was what the chaplain of the Pro-Am tour had said: 'We think we are in the land of the living going to the land of the dying when in reality we are in the land of the dying headed for the land of the living.' When we focus from the beginning on the 'land of the living' all our motives for life seem to distil into a purer form. What do I want to do with my life?

In Revelation God says, 'All who are victorious will inherit all these blessing, and I will be their God, and they will be my children,' (Rev. 21:7). What are the blessings for God's children? Mediate on this:

1)   You will eat from the tree of life (Rev. 2:7).
2)   You will escape from the lake of fire, 'the second death;' (Rev. 2:11).
3)   You will receive a special name (Rev. 2:17).
4)   You will have authority over nations (Rev. 2:26).
5)   Your name will be included in the Book of Life (Rev. 3:5).

6) You will become a pillar in God's spiritual temple (Rev. 3:12).
7) You will be seated with Christ on His throne (Rev. 3:21).
8) You can do all things through Christ, who gives you strength (Phil. 4:13).

We are indeed blessed as children of the King! Don't believe the lies. Don't be deceived. Know with all your heart – WHO YOU REALLY ARE! With that privilege comes both honour and responsibility. Take hold of the truth, and live life like a King's kid!

What good works will I leave behind?

So then, each of us will give an account of himself to God **(Rom. 14:12)**.

What is in my account?

For we are God's workmanship, created in Christ Jesus to do good works, which God prepared in advance for us to do **(Eph. 2:10)**.

Somehow, some way, this is going to happen to you:
You open your eyes in a start and instead of lying next to your spouse of forty years you are bowing before Jesus, you have never seen Him before, He looks little like the blue-eyed painting you stared at in Sunday school class; but you know you are in the presence of Christ in Heaven and your life (true life/new life) is about to begin. He will ask you for 'an account', He prepared 'good works' for you to do; He wants you to build His Kingdom with 'reliable men'. Look back over the last ten years and ask: what account will I give my Master? Look ahead at the next ten years projecting ahead instead of behind, what 'talents' has God given you, what kind of impact can the Lord make through you? I write this after visiting a man close to retirement who poured out his regrets to me in my office. He came feeling wretched and defeated: 'I have wasted so much time – so much time'. I see the love he has for Christ, though he has been a Christian for years it seems as if he has awoken from a half dream-like stupor and realized the enormous sacrifice God has made on his behalf and his lack of appreciation and commitment. Like Ebenezer Scrooge waking up on Christmas day this guy wants to make up for lost time. Did you read that old cliché? Make up for lost time. The past is behind you cannot change it. All the time you have to offer is now before you, time is a gift from God to use for His glory, **what can be a more strategic use of time than to train others to reproduce.** To reproduce – reproducers! 'You then, my son, be strong in the grace that is in Christ Jesus. And the things you have heard me say in the presence of many witnesses entrust to reliable men who will also be qualified to teach others' (2 Tim. 2:1-7). Again let me draw your attention to Robert Coleman's great book *Master Plan of Evangelism*, 'We must decide where we want our ministry to count – in the momentary applause of popular recognition or in the reproduction of our lives in a few chosen people who will carry on our work after we have gone. Really it is a question of which generation we are living for.'

SPORTS OUTREACH

Learning to Disciple when you have Never been Discipled! To Coach when you have Never been Coached.

The key to cohesive sports ministry in the local church is leadership training; 'Go and make disciples!' The Cambodian dictator Pol Pot destroyed his country; his radical communist government displaced millions by forced evacuations of major cities in order to 'cleanse' the Khmer people from external influences. From 1975 to 1979 he systematically killed almost all the educated, educators and over 90 per cent of the small Christian population. He almost completely succeeded. Don Cormack in his eye-witness account documented in *Killing Fields, Living Fields* estimated that only two indigenous Christian leaders survived. On a recent trip to Cambodia I was refreshed to see the growth of a new small, but vital, flock of Christians. There was one sad recognisable quality that I found in both vibrant young Cambodians, and Westerners – they have had to disciple themselves. It is understandable when only two Christian leaders survive a holocaust that young Christians will have to find their way without a shepherd. Is it not criminal that Western youth with such a wealth of Christians at their disposal have to do the same?

Whether or not you have had the experience of good role modelling and mentoring in your life, now is the chance for you to start obeying Christ's Commission to 'Make disciples'. We may not have had earthly role models, but we can follow the example of the disciple-maker, Jesus. In the three years of His public ministry Jesus did many great things. His life had a tremendous impact on countless numbers of individuals. But the major portion of His time was spent with the twelve men in His huddle. Here are some of the ways Jesus made his huddle great: How can you best develop leaders in your sports ministry?

He loved them.
'As the Father has loved me, so have I loved you' (John 15:9).

He prayed for them.
'Holy Father, keep them in thy name, which thou has given me, that they may be one, even as we are one' (John 17:9).

He set an example for them.
'I have set you an example that you should do as I have done for you' (John 13:15).

He shared His victories with them.
'If I go to prepare a place for you, I will come again, and receive you myself; that where I am, there you may be also' (John 14:3).

He shared His hurts with them.
'My soul is deeply grieved to the point of death' (Mark 14:34).

He revealed the truth to them.
'I am the way, and the truth, and the life: No one comes to the Father, but through me' (John 14:6).

He sent them out.
'Go therefore and make disciples of all nations' (Matt. 28:19).

He promised to go with them.
'I am with you always, even to the end of the age' (Matt. 28:20).

*Fellowship of Christian Athletes Training Manual

Recruit - Root - Shoot

 When he saw the crowds, he had compassion on them, because they were harassed and helpless, like sheep without a shepherd. Then he said to his disciples, 'The harvest is plentiful but the workers are few. Ask the Lord of the harvest, therefore, to send out workers into his harvest field.' He called his twelve disciples to him and gave them authority to drive out evil spirits and to heal every disease and sickness (Matt. 9:36-10:1).

In the Gospel of Matthew we see Jesus' ministry of repeatedly healing the sick, blessing the poor and preaching the good news in the synagogues. Then in Matthew 9 you watch Jesus He pauses and seems to be more affected by His children than ever. 'When he saw the crowds, he had compassion on them, because they were harassed and helpless, like sheep without a shepherd. Then he said to his disciples, 'The harvest is plentiful but the workers are few. Ask the Lord of the harvest, therefore, to send out workers into his harvest field.' I ask you do you believe in prayer? Do you really believe that the 'prayers of a righteous man are powerful and effective'? I hope you do. Then let me ask you one more question, if you believe in prayer, do you think that just maybe your ancestors prayed that prayer and missionaries prayed that prayer and perhaps even your grandparents prayed that prayer? So look in the mirror, God is sending you! You are the answer to some old saint's prayers! I don't think it was a coincidence that we find in the next passage of Matthew chapter 10 that Jesus is sending out the twelve on their first missionary journey. Jesus modelled ministry, cast the vision, gave them direct orders, then sent them out to catch some fish.

Recruit:

Understand the great need for Christ and His Kingdom in the lives of those around you and deeply feel for their plight, a life without God. Matthew 9:36 says, 'When he saw the crowds, he had compassion on them. The harvest is plentiful but the workers are few.' Ask God to give you a couple of potential leaders to encourage and challenge. 'Ask the Lord of the harvest, therefore, to send out workers into his harvest field.'

Discipleship is not a programme! It is a life shared in Christ. Spend time together. Most mentoring is a natural process; you cannot reproduce the same teaching and encouragement that Jesus gave His twelve in a Sunday school class. I remember more of my mentors for their attitudes to others while they were driving more than anything they taught me in Sunday school.

Root:

'He called his twelve disciples to him and gave them authority...' (Matt. 10:1).
In Christ you have been adopted into His family enjoying both the inheritance of being a prince and the responsibilities. Instil into those God has given them the 'Great Commission'. God has uniquely gifted the people in your care. Spiritual gifts that are to be used and enjoyed for God's glory you have adopted. 'Continue to live in him, rooted and built up in him, strengthened in the faith as you were taught, and overflowing with thankfulness' (Col. 2:7).

Partnership:

'These are the names of the twelve apostles' (Matt. 10:2).
I have gone to wildly remote places in the world and thought myself the only Westerner around and to my amazement and discouragement I see two clean-cut kids from Utah with white shirts, dark trousers and black bikes riding by. Guess what – the mormons got here first! You never see one it is always two! They use the biblical principle that two is better than one, try not to send out your workers alone. The work is hard, it is lonely we were meant to support each other. The interaction with other leaders can be hard, but partnership is vital. And the good relationships forged are wonderful. Sadly the reason most people leave the mission field is not because of the people they are trying to reach but because of friction among other missionaries. I believe it is because Jesus' next lesson is neglected.

Instructions:

'These twelve Jesus sent out with the following instructions': (Matt. 10:5).
Give your workers clear objectives and clear instructions! Nothing is more frustrating then trying to do a job you are not sure of. What are my aims? Who should I be reaching? How much time do I have? A poor coach can tell you what not to do. It takes a great coach to clearly communicate the objectives before you, then train you and give you training before you are sent into competition. Jesus is not ambiguous; he gives specific targets, guidelines and methodology.

Shoot:

It is no coincidence that after Matthew 9:35, Jesus' methodology progresses from teacher to mobilizer. Before His disciples, Jesus was constantly healing and teaching all those who would come to Him and all who requested Him. We find at verse 35 he stops, has compassion on the lost, encourages prayer for workers, then he prepares and engages his apprentices–

friends in the first short-term mission. Jesus had recruited His disciples, modelled His disciples and now He sends His disciples. The fifth step is messy as He is sending out amateurs who can't do it nearly as well as He can. The third stage is lost in a modern Western church. We get professionals with slick sermons, polished theology and, in many cases, giant egos to entertain us Christians. Entertain, but never send. Graham Daniels, Director of Christians in Sport in the UK says: 'Always training, never playing. How can you get motivated to train hard if you will never get an opportunity to play.' How will someone learn to preach if he cannot get a shot in the pulpit? How will he ever use his apologetics if he never spends time with non-Christians? How can he ever serve if he is not challenged to go? To not send is to nullify the precise Commission we were prepared in advance to do. We must equally share the 'undertaking', and an ordained role (in both the Greek and Hebrew the word 'minister' simply means, 'one who serves') is merely to heighten, train and create opportunities for all Christians to 'undertake' the Commission. It is only the arrogant that think any Christian is exempt from Christian service.

They celebrated:

We need to look at another missionary venture. We see in Luke chapter 10 that Jesus continues to train His future leaders. This time He sends out seventy-two. Let me draw your attention to vs 21 'At that time Jesus, full of joy through the Holy Spirit'. Do you ever see Jesus more happy! He sent out his boys and they tasted the joys of ministry and came back excited. When your people get back from ministry throw them a party! God's people have forgotten how to celebrate! These are blessed festive occasions!

Check List for Reproducing Reproducers:

- Fix their eyes on Jesus and keep the goals before them – vision, be clear about job expectations.
- Be a demonstrator, and a teacher.
- Create a positive friendly atmosphere.
- Create a healthy team. Remember the Lone Rangers usually have their own agendas.
- Have sober expectations about the volunteer's capacity for work.
- Create an atmosphere of appreciation.
- Remember that Satan wants to devour your leadership team.
- Remember everybody is different and will express themselves differently, and that each has unique gifts.
- Remember a volunteer leadership is usually for a period.
- Give loads of encouragement.
- Leaders are on pilgrimage.
- Keep your priority on Christ, not your ministry.
- Build on their strengths, and make the work fun.
- Give them affirmation, affirmation, affirmation.
- Give your leaders authority.

SPORTS OUTREACH

- Accept your own weaknesses.
- Trust in your volunteers.
- Nobody is indispensable!
- You can accomplish almost anything if you are happy not to take credit for it.
- Share the vision with the whole team.
- Celebrate as a whole team.
- Create an expectation that God will work through them.

 For I am already being poured out like a drink offering, and the time has come for my departure. I have fought the good fight, I have finished the race, I have kept the faith. Now there is in store for me the crown of righteousness, which the Lord, the righteous Judge, will award to me on that day – and not only to me, but also to all who have longed for his appearing **(2 Tim. 4:6).**

 His master replied, `Well done, good and faithful servant! You have been faithful with a few things; I will put you in charge of many things. Come and share your master's happiness!' **(Matt. 25:23).**

CHAPTER NINE
SPORTSMANSHIP

ENCOURAGING A CHRISTIAN
SPORTS CULTURE

> *Similarly, encourage the young men to be self-controlled. In everything set them an example by doing what is good. In your teaching show integrity, seriousness and soundness of speech that cannot be condemned, so that those who oppose you may be ashamed because they have nothing bad to say about us* (**Titus 2:6-8**).

WHY is it we can follow the four above principles so closely then completely ignore them in the context of our sports activity? A minister leaned over to me once at a sports banquet with a proud air and confessed, 'It is terrible, but when I play rugby I leave my Christianity on the bench!' His posture of shammed contrition was more of an attempt to evoke applause than to ease his soul. My first impulse was to leave my Christianity in my seat and clock him! If we do not practise good sportsmanship – the character and qualities of Christ manifested in us – in and around the participation of sport, the throat of our gospel message is slashed!

The combination of Christian faith and sport can be so powerful and so misunderstood. It is no wonder that many church leaders resist implementing a sports ministry programme

SPORTS OUTREACH

in their churches. Church leaders are tired of picking up the pieces made from foolish outbursts of unfulfilled sporty parishioners who rationalize their poor sportsmanship as just being 'competitive'. Christians who constantly exhibit bad sportsmanship need to grow up! Interestingly, I see more concern by our pros for living out their Christian faith in competition than by many of our amateurs. Sports ministry can work in every area of sport from the professionals to the church league. We find many brilliant examples of good sports from the highest ranks to the lowest, but for every good example of sportsmanship we often find countless bad examples of poor sportsmanship. Interestingly enough, the bad behaviour exhibited in sport doesn't come from Christian professionals as much as from the recreational and amateur sportsmen, those who are the frustrated 'never really made it class' – the wannabes.

Singing soprano

I asked a pastor-friend of mine who is also a very good athlete (who also very definitely did not want to be named) if he had any examples of good or bad sportsmanship that I could use for this book? My friend kept me laughing for half an hour as I shook my head in disbelief with story after story: he went on to say, '**playing rugby for my Bible college gave me some of the worst experiences I ever had participating in sport**, it was just awful. We studied how to be ministers in the day, but to our shame when we trained or competed for our university, our Christianity seemed to just switch-off! Once during a match a player on the opposing team, (a rival Bible College!) got so frustrated with my roommate that in a broken scrum he grabbed him by the testicles and picked him off the ground! That guy is now a vicar of a big church! And my roommate started singing soprano in the choir!'

While playing golf with an elder of a growing church, I asked him what the church was doing to reach out to the sporting world in their community? He replied sheepishly, 'We had a church team playing in the local secular league.' I said, 'Great how are you doing, are you leading people to Christ, are you making an impact into your community?' The elder replied, 'Well, we made an impact, we were kicked out of the league for fighting.... The clincher was when we punched a ref..' I asked, 'Who was the fool that punched the ref.? Was it someone that does not know Christ, someone you are trying to pull into the church?' The elder turned red and said 'No, I was the fool who punched the ref.'. The stories go on and on. Being an old sportsman these stories seem pretty funny, I have to laugh at my own shortcomings and cringe at my mistakes on the pitch. We often rationalize this behaviour by saying, 'they are just overly competitive.' But in light of Galatians 5:16-24: *'But I say, walk in the Spirit, and do not gratify the desires of the flesh. For the desires of the spirit are against the flesh; for these are opposed to each other, to prevent you from doing what you would... But the fruit of the Spirit is love, joy, peace, patience, kindness, goodness, faithfulness, gentleness and self-control.'* These shortcomings or 'indulgences' in light of Galatians take on the glaring reality of rebellion towards God, or simply – sin.

It is often shocking that some of the most mature Christians, many of whom are leaders in their own churches and are also actively involved in sport, seem to think that they can indulge themselves in improper behaviour in competition. These are people who would never dream of being rude, cheating, fighting or having a temper tantrum in their neighbourhood, place of work, school or church. Why is it that often we feel we have licence to exhibit poor sportsmanship? Sports ministry seeks to identify, implore, train and send out athletes, coaches, and teachers to: 'Reach the world of sport for Christ'. I heard one leader in the sports ministry field say that his dream was to have an 'army of young sports people around the world, to share Christ in the world of sport'. Unfortunately we find Christians seem to turn a blind eye to their own behaviour in sport. If we are to train an army you have to pay attention to detail.

Over-emphasis in sport

Why is it that society will esteem and financially gratify someone who can put a small ball into a hole four hundred yards away with a stick, but underrate and belittle someone who will educate our children or comfort us when we are ill? We can easily be caught in the trap of over-emphasising sport, and undervaluing other facets of life. Winning and losing a match can be dangerously over-emphasised. When we get sport out of proportion, our responses can be equally disproportional.

Andrew Wingfield Digby, founder of Christians in Sport, illustrates the point: 'My son was playing in an under-9s rugby match. We were tied two tries apiece when one of our boys broke away for an impending score, when out of the crowd an opponent's mother (whose husband was the referee) tackled the boy who was certain to score. The game finished in a draw.' Andrew's boy's team was so stunned that they couldn't even oppose the ruling. Finally, questioning the mother's deliberate actions, she replied, 'I couldn't stand losing to you.'

Perhaps you heard of the father who sold his home to finance one of his son's tennis careers, to pay for coaching for the boy in America. The boy, who had shown little more than average ability, was encouraged by his father to become a professional. The father denied any complaint that he was putting undue pressure on his son.

The French scholar and philosopher, Blaise Pascal, once wrote, 'There is a God-shaped vacuum in the heart of every man.' We would certainly never call sport our 'god' but when we put too much emphasis on anything, or rather not enough emphasis on God, our lives become unbalanced, our heart is not being pumped full of life.

SPORTS OUTREACH

SPORTS OUTREACH

Self-sufficiency:

The greatest weakness of mankind, which indeed quite often lends itself to sport, is self-sufficiency. If you train a little bit harder, work a little bit more and push yourself just a bit further then you will succeed in sport and life! If this philosophy works in sport and life, it must certainly be possible to apply it to religion: if you work hard at being a good person, push yourself a bit more to be kind and just a little bit less selfish, then you will make it to heaven. Unfortunately you will be eternally wrong with the self-sufficiency philosophy.

Fortunately you do not have to change, grow and be good to be loved by God! Rather, you are 'loved by God, so that you will change, grow and be good!' Perhaps you should read the last sentence again, especially if you are a rugby player. Ephesians 2:8-9 says, 'For it is by grace you have been saved, through faith and not of yourselves, it is the gift of God, not by works, so that no one can boast.' This is quite a hard concept for someone whose whole life has been governed by the teaching that one succeeds by one's own determination!

Good sport:

Perhaps I am over-emphasising the bad aspect of sport and should now focus on the good. Some people think God's job is finding people who are having a good time them telling them they are not allowed to do it. The truth is God's way is the most fun when we live it by His rules. Looking at some of the problems of sport it is no wonder that the leaders of our churches not so long ago discouraged sporting activity as 'ungodly' and in some cases prohibited sport. But sport can teach us great lessons that will develop our Christian character. Sport has many virtues that can help a young person develop in mind, body and soul, we certainly have to be aware of the pitfalls, but enjoy the benefits.

Team work

Sports ministry should not devalue the mental, physical or social aspects of a person's development. In fact, sport is crucial to developing the social part of the young Christian. Luke tells us that Jesus *'increased in wisdom and stature, and in favour with God and man.* Not just in favour with God, or merely in favour with man. Christ was not a myopic monk concerned only for some deep spiritual event. Nor was he merely a humanist. Christ knew, experienced and understood people. Sport can give us a brilliant opportunity to develop and grow socially.

I worked for several years with Oxford University students, and many of the students couldn't care less about sport. I quite enjoyed my time with the students; many were truly brilliant, energetic and committed Christians and scholars. They were a joy to work with and encourage. But I was always eager to get back to the rest of the day's work with athletes. They are tough, funny, lively and socially amiable. In fact it is usually quite easy to pick out the sports people at the Oxford events. Besides the fact that they are perpetually in sports kit, they are usually laughing the loudest. It is obvious that these students have spent hours working with team-mates adjusting to social pressures like winning and losing.

Humility

'Humility comes before honour' (Prov. 15:33).

'I don't want my young people to have to compete, because they may not perform well and feel terrible.' This was a familiar frustration raised to me as I taught a seminar on 'Sport and Camping' at a national training day for summer camp leaders. I am sure it was out of genuine love for kids that many of the leaders wanted to protect their youth from humiliation. I thought to myself that every one of the leaders who was not in favour of competitive sport probably had an unfortunate humiliating sporting experience in their own lives.

It is indeed a shame when a youngster is unduly humiliated. Yet humility is also a great virtue. Sport often reveals shortcomings and facing up to these can be a valuable lesson. A Dominican monk once wrote, 'He who learns to laugh at himself will never cease to be entertained.' Many sporting experiences are not glorious but they do teach us not to take ourselves too seriously! Romans 12:3 *'Do not think of yourselves more highly than you ought, but rather think of yourselves with sober judgement'*.

Patience and persistence:

'Do not be anxious about anything, but in everything present your requests to God' (Phil. 4:6).

In sport you are constantly waiting and persisting. Whether you are waiting for an injury to heal, persisting through treatment, or waiting for a big match and pushing yourself through training. Sport can teach us to persevere and be patient. A long time Christians in Sport supporter requested prayer at his school's Christian Union meeting with regard to a certain match he was anxious about competing in. The CU leader scorned his prayer request saying, 'We are praying about important things like world peace.' The leader cannot have read Philippians 4:6. 'But in everything present you requests to God' excludes nothing. Christian sports people also need to have patience and perseverance with their brothers and sisters who are not sympathetic to their sport.

Stress:

'So do not fear, for I am with you; do not be dismayed, for I am your God. I will strengthen you and help you; I will uphold you with my righteous right hand' (Isa. 41:10).

You may be shocked that I put 'stress' in the benefit category. I struggled with where to put it myself, until I spoke with a friend who plays semi-professional football and just recently passed his accounting qualifications. He certainly did not walk into the exam centre lightly, but as he observed how uptight others in the exam centre were, he felt quite composed. 'Certainly the lessons I learned on the pitch gave me the ability to give the stress over to God and let him carry me.'

I can not think of anything worse than seeing a parent or a coach screaming at a youth, putting undue pressure on the young person's athletic performance. Nothing will kill a youngster's appetite for competition more quickly than unwarranted stress. Yet there is no better remedy for stress in life than teaching young people to turn their anxieties over to God during sports competition. This can be a valuable experience when a serious crisis strikes their lives.

SPORTS OUTREACH

 'Whatever you do, work at it with all your heart, as working for the Lord, not for men' (Col. 3:23).

'Whatever' includes how we train, perform, and respond to team-mates and competitors. Our Christianity is not just for Sunday morning. Commitment is the ability to adhere your inner and outer self to certain principles or people you value. Scripture says where your treasure is; you will find your heart – your values. If you treasure (value) pleasing God more than men, you are committed to Him. Committing your life to Christ is not easy, but when you value Christ more than anything, you will make a healthy impact on your friends.

In a pro Bible study I attended recently I was happy to hear of one footballer (soccer player) bragging at the example his team-mate was to him. Strangely his team-mate did not quote Scripture nor was he seen to be praying. It was simply his unvarying manner in the locker room. Win or lose he was consistent. Apparently he showed respect for all his team-mates, he was early for training, admitted when he was wrong but moved on, never lingering in self-pity. He said very little, but had the inner confidence that Christians have when they know God is in control of their sport and life. The team soon figured out there was something different about him. Locker rooms can be pretty ungodly places, but retreating from ungodly places is no good. We are called to be salt and light and show Christian principles in all areas of our lives, especially our relationships. When you occupy an area of life with Christian principles, you can turn around institutions from within. No one ever said commitment was easy, but it is powerful.

Reflection
When we see through Jesus' eyes, we love our neighbours and want to do our best.

Prayer
Father, thank you that your love will keep me focused on your ways.

Darkness cannot drive out darkness, only light can do that.
Hate cannot drive out hate, only love can do that.

Dr Martin Luther King

Excerpt from: *A Sporting Guide to Eternity*

Big Seven: Seven Virtues to Infect the World of Sport

I could make a long, long list from experience of what not to do from my past mistakes, but I can never make a list of all the right and wrong ways to conduct yourself in the world of sport. There are too many variables. Besides, that kind of thinking usually digresses into legalism: a sort of religious pride for doing or not doing certain things: Jesus speaks out strongly about that particularly nasty form of sin. Since I can't make a list of what not to do, I thought it would be helpful to leave you with some qualities to enjoy in your sport and in your life. C S Lewis gave a series of radio talks for the BBC during World War II. His subject was Christian behaviour and he suggested the 'seven virtues': **Prudence, Temperance, Justice, Fortitude, Faith, Hope and Love**.

These are a classic Christian list of qualities endowed from God that you develop when God's principles are adhered to. Sadly, good things lose their meaning and this list sounds awfully dull. Satan is good at making really cool things appear to be unappealing and likewise bad things seem really appealing. So let's examine these apparently old fashioned sentiments and see what relevance they have to the sports world. The first four virtues are 'Cardinal virtues'. Cardinal is a Latin word for hinge because on them all lesser virtues hinge: it is not referring to the bird, the baseball team or a Catholic priest. These four virtues are ancient and universal; Christians took these four virtues and added the last three (Theological Virtues'), which the Apostle Paul emphasised. How can these seven virtues help us in sport?

Prudence:

Common sense: in some Christian circles it is not fashionable to be practical. Everything must have a strange aura of mysticism. There is a mystery to God but it does not give us licence to stop using our brain: I am sending you out like sheep among wolves. Therefore be as shrewd as snakes and as innocent as doves – Matthew 10:16. Sometimes we can hide behind Christianity, use it for all types of excuses. As a chaplain I occasionally come across a Christian player who is so caught up in a spiritual fog that they are distracted from being a useful witness. Sometimes the most spiritual thing you can do is to get to training on time!

Temperance:

Self Control: The skill of taking things only as far as what is suitable. Imagine Tiger Woods drops the ball six feet from the ninth hole at St Andrews. He walks up to the green, pulls out a wood and blasts the ball into the North Sea. That is intemperance. God gave us good things to enjoy, not to abuse. We can be intemperate about so many things: sport, clothes, work... Yes there are certain things that are prohibited. There are certain things that are better to stay away from because they will either influence or discourage others. But the attitude is keeping yourself together, to be under control.

Justice:

Fairness: is really important when someone is being unfair to us. But the quality of fairness comes in the measure that we are fair to others: being truthful, keeping our promises, empathy. Playing as hard as you can within the confines of the rules is fair. You may win or lose by one hundred points and someone screams unfair! That is nonsense if both teams agreed to play under the same rules. What is unfair is when you try to win or sometimes lose outside of the rules, or you see a cheat and do not report it. You may choose to play less offensively in order to keep the score under control. But that is more temperance and prudence than fairness.

Fortitude:

Guts: the understanding that we will have trials but in the end we will overcome. We hate pain. Where did we get the notion that in this world we were promised we would enjoy a pain-free life? I wish it were true. In *The Road Less Travelled*, M Scott Peck starts his book by writing, 'Life is difficult', and that is a promise. Sport teaches us to endure the ups and the downs. To stick with it to the end and to endure. It is our hope which gives us our endurance. 'Your endurance inspired by hope in our Lord Jesus Christ' (1 Thess. 1:3).

Faith:

'Now faith is being sure of what we hope for and certain of what we do not see. This is what the ancients were commended for' (Heb. 11:1-2). This is a virtue that needs to be thought out clearly. Faith does not automatically give you virtue. We put our faith in all sorts of things that we shouldn't. If I put my faith in a con man I am pretty stupid. If I put my faith in an unreliable friend I am not very wise. If I put my faith in myself I am a fool. It is where we attribute our faith that is virtuous. I must realize that all I offer God are the flailing hands of a drowning man. Knowing that Christ is the answer to sin and the world and putting your faith in Him is the answer. This quality will free you and help you perform for a higher audience.

Hope:

'We have this hope as an anchor for the soul, firm and secure...' (Heb. 6:19). Long before the 'fish-sign' followers of Christ used an anchor as a symbol of their faith in Christ. In the up and down world of sport what can be more valuable than an anchor? I remember in 1984 in the Chicago Bears locker room when many of the players were cut. I was injured at the time and protected. You could see the emptiness in some of the player's eyes. A fear that said, what is going to happen to me now – is my life over? Yet a few of those players were Christians and though they were deeply disappointed they had an anchor that kept them secure. A security that was far higher than professional sports. No matter what level you play at, disappointment is part of sport but instead of trying to find your happiness in short-term success, Christianity offers permanent joy, we have something wonderful to look forward to.

Love:

'And now these three remain: faith, hope and love. But the greatest of these is love' (1 Cor. 13:13). We can love our spouse, love our friend and love pizza and mean three different things – at least I hope so. The word love was originally charity. The word charity has changed and now conjures up images of the Salvation Army ringing bells at Christmas time and coins being chucked in a bucket. But the original meaning is different. It meant that love is a verb and implied action. When you have love in you the more you use it the more you enjoy it and the better you get at it. This is the key to the rest of the virtues. But the key to love is obedience to God, not trading love for love. That doesn't work because sooner or later someone will not reciprocate your love and you will feel short-changed. But if you love in response and through God's love, you have an eternal power, the true source of love. When I see sports people show love to their team-mates I am filled with pride (the good type). The sports world can be very image conscious and the 'loving image' is not fashionable, so those that break the mould are to me the most secure people on the team.

Closing:

Does sport build character or merely reveal it? The answer is both. Sport is multifaceted. The best and the worst come out when one is under pressure. Fortunately God is in the business of making us better! Paul explains that the attributes of the Spirit are 'fruits'. Many, if not all, of these attributes can be encouraged, learned, developed, fostered or at least exercised through the world of sport.

A note for coaches:

 ## Player vs. Programme

Having a healthy mutual respect for people and task is an art. Do you respect the coach who is successful, and yet who behind-the-scenes is manipulative and is hated by players and colleagues? He might win for a few years but he creates a wake of distrust and disrespect. I always remember my coaches in the long run for their character or lack thereof. I do not remember the championships or the losses – they are all a blur to me now. But the times that a coach came in and took an interest in my injury or family still remain. I remember as a thirteen-year-old sitting in the training room with a badly sprained ankle. The trainer was busy and the Varsity head coach who was a small god in my eyes (at the time) came in and saw my predicament and applied the ice to my ankle himself. There were over 200 kids in the combined American football programmes and I was at the bottom rung. This coach icing my ankle was as close as any act of humility (feet washing act) that I ever experienced. He must have thought I was shuttering at the cold ice on my ankle but it was rather at this man who was taking such a caring interest in me. His equilibrium between person and task (player and sports programme) was mutually beneficial. It is a universal principle. People make teams and teams make people. For Coach Rex it was merely an instinct that manifested itself out of his care for that programme – God had given him a job and that job for him was part task (win football games) and part person (build young men in character and expose them to the Creator). If I asked him about that ankle icing he would never have remembered it. In fact, I doubt that he would remember the record for the year. But that incident and the many more experiences of his care for me as a person meant that I would have done anything for that coach. Nearly thirty years later we are still friends.

CHAPTER TEN
STRATEGY FORMATION

PRINCIPLES THAT
DETERMINE OBJECTIVES

But those who plan what is good find love and faithfulness
(Prov. 14:22).

 Scenario

St Johns Community Church loved the few younger people they had in their greying congregation of about seventy-five regular attendees. Anne, a computer programmer and a delightful new Christian in her mid-twenties, was one of the church's real gems. Her presence always put a smile on the congregation's faces; it made the church feel good about the future seeing a few 'young people' growing in their faith. Anne had gone to the local university and at a Christian meeting gave her life to the Lord. Somehow at the end of her last year of University she ended up going to St Johns instead of the big university church three blocks away. What the church did not know was Anne was an outstanding basketball player. She had represented her University, and was currently playing for a local club team on Tuesday nights. Anne got a job in the city and settled down into a good routine of social life and church activity.

SPORTS OUTREACH

Changes were happening in Anne, she started to blossom as a Christian and over time a seed took root in her mind after hearing a sermon on Mark 1:17: *'Come follow me. I will make you fishers of men.'* She knew instinctively that it was a universal call to outreach and she wanted to get involved. There were shadows of self-doubt as to whether she was 'good enough' for ministry; she certainly did not know as many Scriptures as her pastor and she had never done anything like this before. She also wondered why more people in her church were not responding to the 'call', but did not want to seem judgmental and dismissed the notion. From a gifts assessment test a friend had recently given her she realised she was strong in the areas of leadership and compassion.

Anne's impulse to 'make fishers of men' was formulated while on a rare weekend trip home to visit her mother. Though she did not know anyone at the local church (she became a Christian at University) she cautiously attended, and was pleasantly amazed at how relevant the music was and how open and loving the congregation appeared. This was a mixed blessing as she made the obvious comparison with her own church and found, in some ways, it came up short. What really got her attention was a brochure on the church notice-board that briefly described their sports ministry initiatives and had a photo of local kids playing football. Anne was inspired by the concept, besides hearing of a few professional athletes give a quick Christian blip on television, she really had never thought of sports ministry before. The idea caught her imagination and she found an address of an organisation that would send her a few ideas on how to win the 'world of sport for Christ'. So Anne decided that night to try and start a sports ministry at St Johns Community Church.

How will it play out?

Anne is fictitious but the scenario happens in a countless number of churches. Many wonderful initiatives have started from young and old people earnestly responding to God's challenge to be 'fishers of men'. Sadly, many heart felt initiatives have also died a frustrating and even painful death for lack of preparation. This scenario can play out in a number of ways. Let's break it down into two to illustrate a few points.

Model 1: The Lone Ranger approach

Anne, in her excitement, sets up a meeting with her minister who smiles in an approving but perhaps sceptical way and says 'that's fine, what a wonderful opportunity, go ahead'. She charges out into the world of sport and sets up a mixed club basketball team organised by the church called: 'St John's Saints'. Anne wants to reach her unchurched friends but does not want to frighten them off so she recruits many of her friends and their friends to 'play basket ball and check-out life'. Her friends are not sure what she means by, 'check out life', but the basketball sounds good and Anne is fun to be around.

Anne is now excited about the ministry opportunity and in her mind's-eye sees the church quickly filling with young vibrant students who are worshipping God in a contemporary form. Her first effort at ministry is enthusiastic and she asks the team to pray after a match. Her team-mates feel awkward and stunned, they were not prepared to pray but some unenthusiastically manage a sort of prayerful posture hoping no one is looking and Anne says a quick prayer. She invites the team to church and has three 'takers', all her closest friends; they come, are polite, say 'thanks for the invite' and never come back. Gradually over time Anne is worn down, though she prays quietly for her team the formal team prayers are forgotten, to the relief of the squad. One day after church her minister asks, 'how is our team doing?' Anne replies, 'Oh, it's going great!' – and the minister is happy to hear it, asks no more questions and quickly his mind is on different things. Sadly, her vision of her church filled with a less grey congregation slowly fades and she in two years has let someone else run Saint John's Saints – someone who has never even been to the church.

Model 2: Build a Team approach

Anne, in her excitement, sets up a meeting with her minister. He is busy and terrified that he will have 'one more programme on his schedule', but he sees the enthusiasm in Anne's eyes and deeply wants her to know the enjoyment of being an active Christian. So he challenges her to come back to him in two weeks with a plan on how to have a sports ministry at St Johns. Secretly the minister is sceptical, as he has seen countless parishioners come to his office with well-intended ideas, but without realistic expectations at how hard it will be to develop a healthy sustainable ministry programme. Two weeks seems a ridiculous time to wait for Anne, because she sees the world so lost and wants to reach everyone, today. But she has a good brain and is willing to listen to her minister. With a million ideas in her head, some unworkable, others sound, she starts to formulate a plan. She even gets a copy of other churches' sports ministry prospectuses and develops a strategy including implementing the five principles: Proclamation, Demonstration, Maturation, Reproduction and Sportsmanship. Two weeks later she is back in her pastor's office with an outline suggesting a long-term ministry, and slowly the minister gets interested.

The pastor realises she is serious and wants to help her. He looks at the plan and tries not to laugh, some of the ideas are 'way out there' – like turning the sanctuary into a big sports hall (gym).' But he sees the value in setting up some sports ministry initiatives and he also starts to envision the blessings and headaches that his church full of unchurched athletes may cause. Slowly it dawns on the pastor that there are a few others in the congregation who are sports-minded parishioners. He asks Anne if she knows Jim and Hamish? She doesn't. So he suggests they set-up another meeting in a week. It is actually two weeks because Jim, a former rugby player, is out of town on business. Now it has been a month, Anne is wondering what is taking so long but sees the value in a team and hopes Jim and Hamish will catch the vision... Slowly, over time, a survey on sports interest is put to the church and the new formation committee, Anne, Jim and Hamish, are all surprised at the interest the church members have in sports outreach. A plan is eventually worked out to have a basketball team called St Johns Saints, which is part of a city league and an annual golf event. The minister is pleased, he feels ownership, has a long-term plan and now has three very excited leaders newly engaged in ministry.

Six months later the pastor is accosted in the church hall by Agnes, a retired teacher, who says, 'pastor, why don't we not have a keep-fit programme here for the retired people in the community?' The Pastor smiles and says, 'could you come up with a plan and make an appointment with me and my sports ministry team in two weeks?'...walking away the pastor sighs and thinks: 'I wonder what the sanctuary would look like if we turned it into a basketball court?'

Intentional vs. haphazard

The opposite of intentional is haphazard random ministry: we have, through the years, seen too many earnest ministry initiatives come and go because of poor planning. This section is a guide to help you formulate your own ministry plan and help you mobilise a healthy sustainable sports ministry. Part of *intentional ministry* is having a plan and setting goals. Goals can be intimidating because you create measurable objectives. With clear objectives you now have the ability to gauge your purpose and goals. As mentioned in reproducing reproducers, some Christians bristle at goals and plans saying, 'they are un-spiritual'. I think this is an excuse and am glad Christ modelled strategic discipleship and Kingdom-building. If you aim at nothing you will hit it! Some people can 'wing-it' in ministry, but the quality breaks down like a great natural athlete that tends to coast through their sport – they don't challenge themselves to give their best! Don't settle for mediocrity in ministry, give and model the best effort you can. Create a philosophy of ministry and write out some short and long-term goals. **A goal not written out is merely a wish.**

'For the eyes of the Lord range throughout the earth to strengthen those whose hearts are fully committed to Him' (2 Chron. 16:9).

How to Start a Sports Outreach Ministry

In order for a sports ministry to begin in a church, it takes the vision and support of the senior leaders of your faith community. It is imperative that the leadership (staff and lay leaders) are aware that sports and recreation is a genuine mission field as much as youth-ministry, singles-ministry, music-ministry and other groups to whom the church ministers. Sport is a universal language with the potential for evangelism, discipleship and the enjoyment of Christian fellowship.

Only after the vision for a sports and recreation ministry is fully supported by the leadership should a concerted effort be made to generate interest within the church body (or church bodies if smaller, like-minded churches unite for a common thrust). Next, a nucleus of people should begin to meet with men and women who demonstrate an interest in sport. A response to serve should be accepted only after serious prayer.

Sports Outreach Director:

It is very helpful when developing a sports ministry to identify a key leader who can:
- Organize and supervise leadership teams and direct the planning, operation, and evaluation of the ministry.
- Coordinate the sports ministry activities with church leadership.
- Meet with individual members of the Sports Outreach leadership as often as necessary to help plan, conduct and evaluate each area of assignment.
- Heads leadership team in forming goals and plans for the coming year.
- Determine training needs for the sports ministry leadership team.

Creating a Sports Outreach Mission Plan:

This is a simple examination to help you express your personal goals and ministry objectives.
Section I: is a short questionnaire to see how you personally are doing spiritually; a personal spiritual fitness test. This is meant to be filled out privately. Afterwards, ask yourself, can I share this with anyone?
Section II: is to be filled out with a 'ministry formation team'. Feel free to look at the questionnaire yourself, but if you cannot find anyone to help share the burden of ministry may I suggest you wait until God gives you help. Pray for that help, wait on that help, recruit for that help, but don't start without that help. Try to be as detailed as possible.

Special note: in section II, step three, you will be asked:
- Are our church leaders enthusiastic and supportive for a sports ministry in our church or churches?
- How can we clearly cast a vision for sports ministry to our church leaders?
This process should be started before you get too far down the road, or you may be disappointed.

SPORTS OUTREACH

 Section 1: a Personal Fitness Test!

A closer examination of God's calling and His prerequisites for ministry helps us develop a strategy for achieving God's objectives.

'Here is a trustworthy saying: If anyone sets his heart on being an overseer, he desires a noble task. Now the overseer must be above reproach, the husband of but one wife, temperate, self-controlled, respectable, hospitable, able to teach, not given to drunkenness, not violent but gentle, not quarrelsome, not a lover of money. He must manage his own family well and see that his children obey him with proper respect (If anyone does not know how to manage his own family, how can he take care of God's church?). He must not be a recent convert, or he may become conceited and fall under the same judgment as the devil. He must also have a good reputation with outsiders, so that he will not fall into disgrace and into the devil's trap' (1 Tim. 3:1).

Fill out the first section on your own.

Personal survey:

Before you venture into ministry ask yourself a few questions:

- Am I excited about spending time with God?
- Do I read the Bible regularly?
- Can I clearly share the gospel one-on-one?
- Am I out of sorts with anyone?
- Am I enjoying the company of growing Christians?
- Am I actively seeking a life of integrity and purity?
- What are some of my motives for engaging in ministry? List four.
  -
  -
  -
  -

- Do I want to be involved in the lives of sports people?
- How much time can I give to this initiative?
- Have I really counted the cost of this initiative?
- How many years am I willing to commit to sports ministry in this community?
- Define success in sports ministry?

- What are my strengths?

- What are my weaknesses?

Rate yourself on a scale of 1 – 10   Not very good 1———3——— 5 ———7———10   very good!

•	Am I adaptable?	1———3——— 5 ———7———10
•	Am I good with people?	1———3——— 5 ———7———10
•	Am I dependable?	1———3——— 5 ———7———10
•	Am I good at following through with a plan?	1———3——— 5 ———7———10
•	Am I good at assuming responsibility for a group?	1———3——— 5 ———7———10
•	Am I good at expressing myself?	1———3——— 5 ———7———10
•	Am I good at confronting?	1———3——— 5 ———7———10
•	Am I good working behind the scene?	1———3——— 5 ———7———10
•	Am I good working up front?	1———3——— 5 ———7———10
•	Am I a good planner?	1———3——— 5 ———7———10
•	Am I a good finisher?	1———3——— 5 ———7———10
•	Am I good at challenging myself?	1———3——— 5 ———7———10
•	Am I good at learning new skills?	1———3——— 5 ———7———10
•	Am I good with authority figures?	1———3——— 5 ———7———10
•	Am I good working with children?	1———3——— 5 ———7———10
•	Am I good working with teenagers?	1———3——— 5 ———7———10
•	Am I good working with adults?	1———3——— 5 ———7———10

In light of I Timothy 3:1 has this questionnaire disqualified me from leadership?
- If you answered yes, ask yourself, what can I do to qualify myself for leadership?

- How can I start doing sports ministry?

- Have I lied to myself in this survey? If yes start again!

SPORTS OUTREACH

 ## Section II: Building a Sports Ministry: Getting Ministry from Alpha to Omega:

This section is designed to be worked through by a sports ministry formation team. Feel free to look at the questionnaire yourself, but if you cannot find anyone to help share the burden of ministry may I suggest you wait until God gives you help. Pray for that help, wait on that help, recruit for that help, but don't start without that help.

66 Special note for ongoing sports ministries

Lets face it, you are probably involved in sports ministry already or you have a pretty good idea what you want to do. I am occasionally asked to help 'fix' a church's ongoing sports ministry which is not achieving its objectives; the biggest problem usually is: 'How do you integrate the people from the pitch (field, for my North American brothers) to the church? We do church and we have a sports team but nothing is really happening, we can't get them together.' Creating a cohesive sports ministry takes work. If your sports ministry is flagging, this process will help you to re-evaluate and re-tool. This process will focus your priorities and transform your ideas and Christian values into action and healthy strategic activities. This process also helps you tailor a biblically centred programme for your specific community. I suggest you do this in a couple of stages so you can reflect on and pray through the exercise.

Step 1

Examine the five principles again: following this process will keep you on course and be more strategic. This process usually eliminates some candidates for leadership that really only want to do the activity and not the ministry. Is your activity a ministry or a baby-sitting service? Baby-sitting is fine but it is not ministry. Ask yourself what is important?

Building a ministry:

Build a foundation for your ministry by examining the biblical foundation, principles; create ministry objectives that shape ministry activities.

Proclamation: *verbalisation of truth*
And how can they believe in the one of whom they have not heard? And how can they hear without someone preaching to them? And how can they preach unless they are sent? (Rom. 10:14-15).

Demonstration: *visualisation of truth*
Question: 'Teacher, which is the greatest commandment in the Law?'
Answer: Jesus replied: "Love the Lord your God with all your heart and all your soul and with all your mind.' This is the first and greatest commandment. And the second is like it: 'Love your neighbour as yourself.' All the Law and the prophets hang on these two commandments.'
Question: 'And who is my neighbour?'
Answer: The expert of the law replied, 'The one who had mercy on him.'
Action: Jesus told him, 'Go and do likewise.'

Maturation: *cultivation of truth: nourish: to provide all that is necessary for growth.*
'To prepare God's people for works of service, so that the body of Christ may be built up until we all reach unity in the faith and in the knowledge of the Son of God and become <u>mature</u>, attaining to the whole measure of the fullness of Christ' (Eph. 4:12).
Incubation + Education + Application = Maturation

Reproducing reproducers: *Building leaders who can build leaders.*
'And the things you have heard me say in the presence of many witnesses, entrust to reliable men who will also be qualified to teach others' (2 Tim. 2:2).
What reliable people have I poured my life into?

Sportsmanship: *Encouraging a Christian sports culture*
'Similarly, encourage the young men to be self-controlled. In everything set them an example by doing what is good. In your teaching show integrity, seriousness and soundness of speech that cannot be condemned, so that those who oppose you may be ashamed because they have nothing bad to say about us' (Titus 2:6-8).

SPORTS OUTREACH

Step 2
Team ministry formation survey:

- How can a sports ministry contribute to our church?

- What are the sports of interest in our community? (It might help to survey your church for potential leaders and interest).

- What are the ages?

- What is our target audience?

- How can we meet our target audience?
  Contact points:
    - health club
    - sports clubs
    - leagues
    - schools
    - universities

- How can we build momentum in our sports ministry? (See chapter 11.)

- How can we proclaim the gospel to our target audience?

- How can we demonstrate the gospel to our target audience?

- How can we build a climate for Christian maturity for our target audience?

- How can we identify and build leaders into our ministry?

- How can we maintain a quality of good sportsmanship in our ministry?

Step 3

Transforming principles into action:

'Since you are my rock and my fortress, for the sake of your name lead and guide me' (Ps. 31:3).
Work backwards to forwards. Start with a dream, a vision, a result and work backwards. Many evangelistic events have little planning or expectation and become merely a series of proclamations with very little preparation or forethought for growing a young Christian or ministry. So work backwards. Remember most people plan too much in one year and not enough in five. Imagine where you want to be in five years. Ask God to give you a dream and vision.

Imagine:

What could a new Christian look like if they had been genuinely encouraged to grow spiritually over four or five years? Would they be able to find strength from the Bible? Would they be able to comfortably pray with others? Could they encourage others to stand strong in Christ? Would they be able to share their faith with others? Could they be planning a ministry of their own? Could they be mature enough to demonstrate Christian grace even after losing in public? Could they break bad habits? It happens all over the world but rarely by accident. Many young Christians have blossomed because they have found themselves in an environment that will challenge them and help them to mature. Someone has cultivated their garden.

 ## Scenario

Imagine what a golf ministry could look like in your church five years from today and work your way back.

Five years after starting their church's sports ministry one church reported two evangelistic golf tournaments (spring and autumn).

• The **spring** tournament hosted 75 participants, it was a fundraiser for their orphanage in Cambodia, the evangelism was informal, and Christian booklets were passed out.

• The **autumn** tournament was a smaller group – 45 participants and a clear evangelistic message was given after the dinner.

• From that dinner they had six people come to their eight week Sports Outreach Discovery Team, which has seen fifty-five people go through in the past five years.

• Their fellowship group is still meeting on the first Saturday of the month, which includes a Bible study and, weather permitting, a round of golf.

• Another spin-off from last year is their weekend away. Sixteen couples came this year; they played four rounds of golf and had an optional bible study at night. Half the participants were unchurched guests. It was compulsory that if you were from their church you had to invite another couple outside the church and attend their 'how to give away your faith' four week course.

• Lastly they are sponsoring two of the young high school leaders to attend with two of their unchurched golf buddies, a national Christian sports camp.

Why long-term planning?

You may look at the above list and think no problem; we could do that in one year. You may look at the above list and think it would take a lot longer than five years to achieve. I don't know your church, but the above is an example of a very average church implementing their sports ministry over five years.

Long-term planning, training your leadership and focusing on fulfilling your biblical purposes are crucial for a healthy cohesive ministry. Oh, did I mention it also needs prayer,

SPORTS OUTREACH

prayer and more prayer! Most ministries burn out when the ministry is directed by a one-man show. Off they go with the whole ministry riding on them. When they are done the ministry is done. Build leaders, keep focused and have patience. Rick Warren's book *The Purpose Driven Church* has encouraged countless people to think out a cohesive strategy for ministry. He gives a wonderful illustration that I have heard quoted by several Christian leaders around the world. 'Of all the growth patterns I've observed as a gardener, the growth of the Chinese bamboo tree is the most amazing to me. Plant a bamboo sprout in the ground, and for four or five years (sometimes much longer) nothing happens! You water and fertilize, water and fertilize – but you see no visible evidence that anything is happening. Nothing! But about the fifth year things change rather dramatically. In a six-week period the Chinese bamboo tree grows to be a staggering ninety feet tall!'

Opposition:
Your plans will change and be adapted in time. You may be embarrassed by not planning enough or feel overwhelmed by planning too much. Remember this is an exercise to help you project and cast a vision and then act in faith. You will get opposition from both sides, flack from the flock and those outside the church. You won't be the first. Read Nehemiah 4, remember Nehemiah against all odds was commissioned by God to rebuild the walls of Jerusalem (which he did in fifty-two days). Listen to those like Tobiah that mocked his efforts. 'What they are building – if even a fox climbed up on it, he would break down their wall of stones!' Nehemiah replied in prayer, 'Hear us, O our God, for we are despised'...'So we rebuilt the wall till all of it reached half its height, for the people worked with all their heart'. You will have grumblers and sceptics who will tell you that if a fox climbed your ministry it would tumble! Stay focused, work with all your heart and be obedient, and watch what our powerful Lord can do.

Step 4
Refining our objectives

Can we create a sports ministry that:
- proclaims biblical truth? (How?)
- is an example of servanthood and a means of fellowship?(How?)
- creates a system for discipleship?(How?)
- builds strong leaders? (How?)
- is a challenging, healthy and fun environment? (How?)

- Are our church leaders enthusiastic and supportive of a sports ministry in our church or churches?

- How can we clearly cast a vision for sports ministry to our church leaders?

- How can we integrate a sports ministry into our local church or community of churches?

- How many more leaders can we recruit to help us? List them and start praying for them!

- How best can we cast a vision for a sports ministry to our congregation?

- How can we train our sports ministry leaders?

- How much time will it cost?

- How much time can we afford?

- Have we considered the prep time not just the activities?

- List twenty objectives. Dream! (Separate sheet- but save it.)

- List your top five long-term sports ministry objectives.

- Do we have a plan for staying focused? List four ways.

- What might it look like in five years?

As well as bigger outreach events, it is important to offer regular growth opportunities for fellow Christians. Sports Outreach Team meetings are the heart of the whole ministry concept. A 'Sports Outreach Team' is like a 'huddle': an American football term whereby a team gathers together on the pitch in a small circle and discusses various plays and strategy. A Sports Outreach Team meeting is a small group committed to investigate the scriptures in the context of their sport and life in eight week sessions. (See Appendix 8)

We have a series of three team meetings:
Sports Outreach: Discovery Teams
Sports Outreach: Impact Teams
Sports Outreach: Leadership Teams

- **Discovery Teams** are geared for those that have experienced a camp or outreach event and want to commit to investigating the claims of Christ.
- **Impact Teams** aim to challenge and develop the believer to a stronger walk in Christ.
- **Leadership Teams** seek to challenge and train Christians to be active and fully committed followers of Christ: able to reproduce reproducers.

SPORTS OUTREACH

What Could Your Ministry Look Like in Four Years?

Year 1

	Outreach	Sports Outreach Team (small groups)
January:	Sport Training Conference	Leadership Team
February:		Leadership Team
March:	Sports Quiz Night	
April:		
May:		
June:	Football Tournament	
July:	Sport Camp	
August:	Ten Mile Walk	
September:	Family Open Gym	Discovery Team
October:		Discovery Team
November:		Impact Team
December:	Coaching Clinic	Impact Team

Year 2

	Outreach	Sports Outreach Team (small groups)
January:	Sport Training Conference	Leadership Team
February:		Leadership Team
March:	Sports Quiz Night	
April:	Golf Outreach	
May:		
June:		
July:	Sport Camp	
August:	Ten Mile Walk	
September:	Family Open Gym	
October:	Sports Guest Service	
November:		Impact Team
December:	Coaching Clinic	Impact Team

Year 3

Outreach		Sports Outreach Team (small groups)
January:	Sport Training Conference	Leadership Team
February:	Outreach Dinner	Leadership Team
March:		
April:	Golf Outreach	
May	Night of Champions	Impact Team
June:		Impact Team
July:	Sport Camp	
August:	Ten Mile Walk	
September:	Family Open Gym	Discovery Team
October:	Sports Guest Service	Discovery Team
November:		
December:	Coaching Clinic	

Year 4

Outreach		Sports Outreach Team (small groups)
January:	Sport Training Conference	Leadership Team
February:	Outreach Dinner	Leadership Team
March:	Sports Quiz Night	Discovery Team
April:	Golf Outreach	Discovery Team
May:	Night of Champions	Impact Team
June:	Football Tournament	Impact Team
July:	Sport Camp	
August:	Ten Mile Walk	
September:	Family Open Gym	Discovery Team
October:	Sports Guest Service	Discovery Team
November:	Match Day	Impact Team
December:	Coaching Clinic	Impact Team

SPORTS OUTREACH

Sports Outreach Events: Activities that can Achieve your Objectives

Planning Guide: Suggestions and Checklist

Prayer: human efforts do not produce divine results!
Prayer is the prerequisite to any Christian event! It would be hard for you to over-do prayer. Action-oriented sports people can find it difficult to give time to effective prayer. Discipline yourself to be proactive pray-ers rather than reactive pray-ers!
- Find prayer support in your local church.
- Inform neighbouring churches and solicit their prayerful support.
- At organising meetings don't rush a quick prayer at the end, begin with prayer and listen expectantly for God's voice and direction.
- Have a prayer team meet during the event.

Be organised: 'The artistic temperament is a disease that inflicts amateurs and the ill-prepared' (GK. Chesterton). Organize your event well. It is better to do one event with quality than four events poorly. Again an event can be three people at a house or restaurant or a huge gathering in a stadium, either way, plan ahead.

Evaluation: Prepare a time in advance for post-event evaluation.
- Knowing the evaluation process is looming helps keep you and your team focused on the objectives.
- Be careful when you debrief: this is a time of reflection and coaching not a time of criticism.
    - The best debrief is reflective. Give it a few days. Rarely do I debrief right after an event. I am usually too tired and want to go home.
    - If I have a big team to debrief I send them home with a form. That way if they really want to make an evaluation they will put out the energy to fill it out and send it back.
    - Listen to your leaders and learn, some critique will be inappropriate but much will be valuable. When your leaders see you listening and modifying your work your volunteers will feel more valued and apt to listen to you.

Build a team:
- Building a team is not just picking capable people and sending them into the work. Don't get ahead of yourself. Building a team is sports ministry! This takes time but will produce a strong foundation (Chapter 8).
    - Have you trained them?
    - Do they understand the five principles of sports ministry?

- Are they open to ministry coaching?
- Have they been taught to comfortably communicate their faith informally?

- Reproducing: putting the people you are ministering to into roles of responsibility is one of the best ways for them to grow and mature into strong leaders. This is a sensitive job and needs serious consideration. Challenging your leaders is brilliant, overwhelming your leaders is ruinous.
  - You can get a lot more accomplished if you are willing to let someone else take the credit for it.
- Recruit help, these are great opportunities to mobilise young Christians and identify new leaders for ministry.
- Multichurch events: often two or three churches together can organize something better than one church. This is also a great witness for unchurched people who may perceive that denominations are divided.
- Balance: you may want to bring in some unchurched leaders into the coaching roles. This can be a great opportunity for proclaiming Christ and demonstrating the gospel. It is a delicate decision and the coaches will need to be prepared for coaching in a Christian environment.

Introducing the
Sports Outreach Principle Scale:

- Examine the five principles and determine your objectives accordingly. Events are varied and can give you great opportunities to focus on different principles of ministry.
  - Most good events will incorporate all five principles at various levels. Again proclamation without demonstration is poor evangelism. Concurrently demonstrating the gospel without ever proclaiming the truth is poor ministry. The below is the Sports Outreach Principle Scale. When planning an event check the principle you want to cover and the emphasis you want to achieve.
    - For instance: you may plan a golf outing. It may be appropriate to have a gentle epilogue approach but not a full-blown proclamation. But you may have just trained two or three of your young leaders to share their faith one-on-one and want to create opportunities for them to share. You would circle low formal, high informal, and high maturation and reproduction.
    - Eventually the practice will become second nature and you will rarely need to look at the principle scale.
      - Remember though it may be second nature to you, don't assume your leadership team knows your objectives unless you convey them clearly and agree on them.

SPORTS OUTREACH

Planner

Principles determine method:

Sports Outreach Principle Scale: Low emphasis   High emphasis

- Proclamation: Verbalisation of truth
  - Formal Proclamation   0 – 1 – 2 – 3 – 4 – 5
  - Informal Proclamation   0 – 1 – 2 – 3 – 4 – 5
- Demonstration: Visualization of truth.   0 – 1 – 2 – 3 – 4 – 5
- Maturation: Nourishment of truth.   0 – 1 – 2 – 3 – 4 – 5
  - Incubation: 0 – 1 – 2 – 3 – 4 – 5
  - Education: 0 – 1 – 2 – 3 – 4 – 5
  - Application: 0 – 1 – 2 – 3 – 4 – 5
- Reproduction: Reproducing reproducers.
  - Training: 0 – 1 – 2 – 3 – 4 – 5
  - Application: 0 – 1 – 2 – 3 – 4 – 5
- Sportsmanship: Encouraging a Christian sports culture. 0 – 1 – 2 – 3 – 4 – 5

Carry on and follow up:

- Shouldn't this be at the end of the planner? It depends on if you are committed to a cohesive ministry or merely a series of events. Lack of follow-up is where the many hours of preparing a good evangelistic event can be wasted. Follow-up should not be an afterthought. Think through and develop a long-term strategy.
- I suggest that before you plan your event you plan your follow-up strategy, for instance a Sports Impact Team (see appendix 7 on 'Sports Impact Teams' (Small Groups) and put a few possible dates in place before you go too far into your event planning.
- When an athlete indicates that they have interest in spiritual things, make a personal contact with them – preferably in the next couple of days.
  - Send them a letter and a sports testimony tract; this can be a lifeline for somebody considering the Christian faith.
    - Invite them to your church.
    - Invite them to a fellowship.
    - Invite them to attend a Sports Impact Team.

Programming: pulling on the same side of the rope:

- Identify your objectives and clearly communicate them to the rest of your leaders. Remember an event is only part of the whole ministry. Usually an event can achieve more than one objective, but having specific expectations helps your leaders focus.
  - How does this event contribute to the whole of our sports ministry?
  - Is this an event we want to sustain or merely a one-off?
  - Should we do this:
    1. annually
    2. quarterly

3. bimonthly
4. weekly
5. once a term
6. every Olympics or World Cup?

- Proclamation – formal or informal:
  - Decide whether your event will have formal proclamation or simply a relationship-building approach. A decision needs to be made as to whether or not to have a *formal* Christian proclamation or leave it to your trained team to share informally. Sometimes the gentle approach is more powerful. This is often called '**pre-evangelism**' and helps warm up your athletes to the concept of sports outreach. Do not be afraid to simply provide good coaching and fellowship. This approach gives credence to a more formal evangelistic sporting event later. Either way, after this type of event the Christian stereotype is usually changed, which can provide future gospel opportunities.

- Plan a varied programme:
  - competition
  - coaching
  - music
  - drama
  - testimonies

- The events should be sports-oriented but do not be afraid of asking your local Christian drama or music groups for help. Music and drama should be concise, pointed and well-rehearsed.
  - Communicate your aims to the dramatist and musicians clearly to avoid embarrassment and frustration.

- If you have a speaker (read The Good Christian Guide: How to Treat a Speaker, Appendix 2)
  - Clearly define what you expect of them.
  - Have speakers link the theme into the their talk.
  - Understand the speaker's strengths and weaknesses, quite often local Christian sporting figures are happy to be interviewed but will not be comfortable presenting an evangelistic message.
  - The MC (Master of Ceremonies) is important for creating an atmosphere for the speaker (See appendix 1 for details).

- A clear testimony by one or two of the young people will speak volumes to their peers. Be sensitive as to who you choose, but do not be afraid to encourage some of the most unlikely characters, this may be exactly what they need to mature in Christ.

SPORTS OUTREACH

- If you are running a coaching clinic and have a suitable coach, provide an opportunity during the session for them to relate their faith to their sport.
- Give your coach clear guidelines and advanced notice.
- Provide a good venue for speaking and listening.

- Meeting themes can be quite useful; Jesus drew the attention of His followers by creating parables from everyday life. A pithy and provocative title can stimulate curiosity, i.e... 'The Big Foul', 'Break Point', 'Fit for Life'.
- Did I mention prayer? Human efforts do not produce divine results! See Chapter 4.

 Logistics

I remember running a Night of Champions in Northern England. Everything was running smoothly until our fifteen-minute break time. I turned the corner and saw three hundred testy youths waiting while two old grannies tried to serve them all tea! I totally blew it by forgetting to plan well for the break. The event timing went totally out of kilter because of one simple oversight!

Logistics is servanthood: having people prepared to work hard at making everything run smoothly. Run through an event from the eyes of your guest.
- Is it clear where to go?
- Have they been warmly greeted?
- Did I mention prayer?
- Is the registration line manned properly?
- Will the programme run smoothly?
- Are the facilities suitable?
- Are there ample facilities for water or toilet breaks?
- Was there ample and quality coaching time (when appropriate)?
- Are the competitions smoothly organised and refereed?
- Is there first aid available (when appropriate)?
- Are the prizes appropriate?
- Will the refreshments be quality?
- Will it end on time?

Create a budget:
- Decide whether this event will create revenue or be completely sponsored. I find when youth events are completely sponsored the youth do not value the event as much as if a small fee is charged. When an event is planned and organized well it is worth going to. I recommend that if this is a special 'youth-event', even if it is subsidised by a church or community of churches, you consider with your organising

team charging a fee. It may be a nominal entrance fee but it has been my experience that if you let them in for free, it will be of no value to them. If the youth genuinely cannot afford the entrance fee, create work for them. Involve them in handing out publicity, cleaning up, etc....

- Remember sports people are used to paying to participate in sport. This is a potentially touchy subject, but you will know how to best fund your local ministry.

- Possible expenses:
    - Facility hire
    - Media equipment
    - Refreshments
    - Insurance
    - Sports amenities (T-shirts, sports bags, water bottles, etc.)
    - Spiritual materials
    - Speaker's fee
    - Christian literature (magazines, Bibles, tracts)

- Possible revenue:
    - Church Sports Ministry budget
    - Individual donors
    - Corporate sponsors

Meeting your community's needs:

Discover by questionnaire what events might be popular in your community. You may be a mad about synchronised swimming but you might have little uptake for it. Perhaps you should consider an event based around golf or football. Chapter 11 will give you some suggestions for events where a formal proclamation could take place.

Take sport seriously:

This is the best way to develop sportsmanship. There are wonderful ministries out there for the casual participant in sport. But a serious athlete can be frustrated and insulted by you or your leaders if you don't approach their sport seriously. There are different skill levels, this is usually unavoidable; a serious sportsman is used to dealing with that particular challenge all the time, but not with a lackadaisical attitude to the sport.

- Teach skills of particular sports using local Pros, PE teachers and qualified coaches. Show you are serious about sport and not trying to manipulate your guests with 'bait and switch tactics'.
    - Solid coaching
        - Instruct
        - Model
        - Drill
        - Compete
    - Be prepared for a variety of skill levels.

SPORTS OUTREACH

- Remind your coaching staff of the quality and approach you want to take in your events (Review chapter 9).
- Organization of time-tables, round-robin competition, tee-off times and specific rules are vital to the integrity of your event.

Publicity:

- This is the era of information overload. If your publicity is quality, people will expect your meeting to be quality.
- The best publicity is word of mouth, one friend inviting another. Don't rely on a famous name or media advertising. **If your core group is incapable of bringing a friend you have some serious problems.** Consider a much smaller event and training and recruiting leaders. See chapter 5 on informal proclamation.
- Posters and handbills will reflect the quality of your meeting and create an impression of your group.
    - Be fussy and double check your details: when, where, age, activities, venue…
    - Use catchy, relevant titles and make it clear it is run by a church or Christian organisation. It would do more damage to get youth there under false pretences than to not have them at all!

Comment cards: See Appendix 4

- What did you think of the event?
- Did the talks make any sense to you?
- Are you interested in spiritual things?
- Have you asked Christ into your life?
- Would you like to?
- Would you like more information?
- Would you be interested in joining an eight-week Discovery Team training course for athletes? We have three courses called Discovery Teams, Impact Teams and Leadership Teams available under the Sports Outreach heading. See the back of this book for details.

Thank your workers:

- Set aside time to thank and show appreciation to all those that have come to help.
    - A phone call or letter will go miles towards keeping your leaders enthused, encouraged and feeling valued.
    - Christ showed great pleasure when His disciples came back from ministry experiences. This is a great opportunity to encourage and build your 'reproducers'!

CHAPTER ELEVEN
MODELS OF SPORTS MINISTRY

OBJECTIVES DETERMINE ACTIVITIES

 The idea seemed good to me; so I selected twelve of you, one man from each tribe... **(Deut. 1:23).**

IN this chapter we want to show you some healthy examples of Sports Outreach. Obviously you have to adapt them to your own church culture.

There is a lot of repition in the models because we have tried to adapt the principles to each different event – this way you can use the layout for each event without missing any of the components needed to minster with excellence. For more help on using the material, or staging any of the events, please see our website – www.sportsoutreach.com

SPORTS OUTREACH

Church Sports Service

Planner

Purpose: to share Christ with our sports community and give our church members involved in sport an opportunity to bring their friends and team-mates. The sports service is aimed at people to embrace Christ and 'participate' in the local church. Therefore a sports service should be geared to non-Christian sports people who may have a poor conception of church. Set up a prayer network and inform your congregation as to the nature of the outreach. Encourage a simple, clear service. Have a short and sharp testimony; a local Christian sports personality can be much more powerful than a 'Big' personality. Point the whole service to the power of the cross and not towards man. Encourage the speaker to apply his presentation of the Gospel to an audience that understands sport. Again strong thought-out follow-up!

It could be an annual event until you have enough people to make it biannual. It could also serve to highlight a Sports Outreach Dscovery Course.

Principles determine method:

Sports Outreach Principles Scale.	Low emphasis	High emphasis
• Proclamation: Verbalisation of truth		
• Formal Proclamation	0 – 1 – 2 – 3 – 4 – 5	
• Informal Proclamation	0 – 1 – 2 – 3 – 4 – 5	
• Demonstration: Visualization of truth.	0 – 1 – 2 – 3 – 4 – 5	
• Maturation: Nourishment of truth.	0 – 1 – 2 – 3 – 4 – 5	
• Incubation:	0 – 1 – 2 – 3 – 4 – 5	
• Education:	0 – 1 – 2 – 3 – 4 – 5	
• Application:	0 – 1 – 2 – 3 – 4 – 5	
• Reproduction: Reproducing reproducers.		
• Training:	0 – 1 – 2 – 3 – 4 – 5	
• Application:	0 – 1 – 2 – 3 – 4 – 5	
• Sportsmanship: Encouraging a Christian sports culture.	0 – 1 – 2 – 3 – 4 – 5	

Prayer and Planning: See:' Sports Ministry Events' Planning Suggestions and Checklist
- Core group monthly prayer/planning meeting.
- Inform churches and intercessory team of this initiative.
- Pray daily for the outreach and for those who will attend.
- Pray during church services for the outreach event.
- Encourage your sports ministry group to bring their friends and team-mates.
- Create an invitation to be presented to friends personally.
- Create a poster to display in sports halls, gyms and churches.
  - Write up an announcement for the local newspaper.
- This particular outreach usually needs no specific age group target.

Carry-on and follow-up plans:
- Invite them to a Sports Outreach Discovery Team.
- Invite them to a sports camp or mini-camp.
- Invite them to your house for lunch.

Programme:
- **Order of Service:**
  - Greeters at the door with a video (e.g. *More than Gold*) playing in the sanctuary with contemporary Christian music being dubbed in the background.
- **Music:** choose choruses or hymns which many people may have heard before. Choose words which preach Christ, and don't involve a response from the singer which unchurched people might not know or believe. For instance, don't choose 'I believe in Jesus' or 'I am a new creation'.
- **Media:** Show a clip from a sports event where there was both anger and joy.
- **Sketches:** Create a sketch about pinning all your hopes for happiness on winning.
- **Offering:** Remind whoever calls for the uplifting of the offering to be sensitive to their guests. When I have guests come to my house for dinner I don't ask them to pay for it during the dessert.
- **Other Ideas –**
  - Have someone who has gone through your Sports Outreach training course to announce to the rest of the church you will be starting a new course and give testimony to the value of taking the course.
  - Ushers could wear their favourite sporting gear?
  - Create a finish line in the sanctuary.
  - You could possibly try a short bike race up the aisle during the children's talk?
  - Measure the distance of Jonathan Edwards's world record triple jump (18.29m) up the aisle. Emphasise God has given us a body that is remarkable and to be used to glorify Him.
- **Testimony** by local athlete.
- **Message:** could I suggest the *Sports Outreach Topical Bible* for ideas.
- **Music:** The music group could perform one or two songs that were relevant and evangelistic.
- **Invitation:** to pray together after the service.
  - Remind them to sign up for Sports Impact course.

SPORTS OUTREACH

Specialist Coaching Clinic

Planner

Purpose:

- To attract people within your area that would not be interested in other Christian events, by means of specialist coaching in sport.
- To give your sports ministry group an opportunity to reach out to serious sports people.
- To provide an enjoyable opportunity to provide sports coaching where the gospel can be proclaimed in a relevant manner.
- This could easily be an annual or biannual event, rotating a major sport during its off-season one year and a combination of sports and recreation the next.
- To provide exposure to various uncommon sports and give opportunities to learn new skills – such as fly-casting.

    For example:

    - First year: Soccer
    - Second year: Combination: fly-casting, rock climbing, tennis and golf
    - Third year: Basketball
    - Fourth year: Combination: cart racing, javelin throw, canoeing and mountain biking

Principles determine method:

Sports Outreach Principles Scale.

	Low emphasis High emphasis
Proclamation: Verbalisation of truth	
• Formal Proclamation	0 – 1 – 2 – 3 – 4 – 5
• Informal Proclamation	0 – 1 – 2 – 3 – 4 – 5
Demonstration: Visualization of truth.	0 – 1 – 2 – 3 – 4 – 5
Maturation: Nourishment of truth.	0 – 1 – 2 – 3 – 4 – 5
• Incubation:	0 – 1 – 2 – 3 – 4 – 5
• Education:	0 – 1 – 2 – 3 – 4 – 5
• Application:	0 – 1 – 2 – 3 – 4 – 5
Reproduction: Reproducing reproducers.	
• Training:	0 – 1 – 2 – 3 – 4 – 5
• Application:	0 – 1 – 2 – 3 – 4 – 5
Sportsmanship: Encouraging a Christian sports culture.	0 – 1 – 2 – 3 – 4 – 5

Prayer and Planning: (See 'Sports Ministry Events' Planning Suggestions and Checklist)

- Core group monthly prayer/planning meeting.
- Inform churches and intercessory team of this initiative.
- Pray daily for the outreach and for those that will attend.

- Pray during church service for the outreach event.
- Target specific age groups and skill levels.
- Encourage your sports ministry group to bring their friends and team-mates.
- Create an invitation to be presented to friends personally.
- Create a poster to display in sports-halls, gyms and churches.
    - Make it clear that this includes Christian content when appropriate.
    - Be disciplined about pre-booking.

Carry-on and follow-up plans:
- Invite your friends to your church's next guest service.
- Invite them to a Sports Outreach Discovery Team.
- Invite them to a sports camp or mini camp.
- Invite them to dinner

Programme:
Special note: Sports clinics provide an opportunity for athletes to develop their sport. This book is written for a number of different cultures, countries and sports. You will know your particular sport far better than I ever will. Your qualified coaches will know the best way to provide coaching clinics within the facilities and time restraints you have. All I can say is be creative, provide the best coaching you can. You may be the only Christian your participant knows and the integrity of your programme will speak volumes to them. Some skills are tough to build with a small group – I remember my first sports camp in England for Christians in Sport. Bryan Mason, director of Church Sports Ministry (who has forgotten more about church sports ministry than I know), was my rugby coach: he had only two prop forwards, one was sixteen years old and ninety kilos the other prop was twelve and no bigger than the ball. I don't know what he did with those kids all week but they grew and looked very tired!

Consider:
- Decide on whether you want to have several clinics where the group can rotate through various sports or just one. Provide opportunities for competitions and prizes, i.e.... the best out of five chip shots into a dustbin (indoor balls) on the other side of the sanctuary wins a cap or a bar of chocolate.
- Numbers of participants.
- Possible skill level.
- Will you provide opportunities for competition or merely instruction.
- Basic skills
- Advanced skills
- Individual and team strategy
- Video instruction and/or review (replay drills or competition)
- Personal evaluation and fitness programmes

SPORTS OUTREACH

Requirements:

Qualified coaches and necessary facilities. Facilities can often be improvised. For example, organized golf lessons have taken place in winter months. All you need is a few mats, a net and some plastic practice golf balls, and the church has been turned into an improvised golfing range.

Christian content:

A decision needs to be made as to whether or not to have a *formal* Christian proclamation (epilogue). Do not be afraid to simply provide good coaching and fellowship. This approach gives credence to a more formal evangelistic sporting event later. Either way, after this type of event the Christian stereotype is usually changed, which can provide future gospel opportunities.

Golf Outreach

Planner

Purpose:
- To give your sports ministry group an opportunity to reach out to their golfing community.
- To expose unchurched men and women to Christian fellowship.
- To create opportunities for informal and formal proclamation of the gospel.

Principles determine method:

Sports Outreach Principles Scale		Low emphasis	High emphasis
• Proclamation:	Verbalisation of truth		
• Formal Proclamation		0 – 1 – 2 – 3 – 4 – 5	
• Informal Proclamation		0 – 1 – 2 – 3 – 4 – 5	
• Demonstration:	Visualization of truth.	0 – 1 – 2 – 3 – 4 – 5	
• Maturation:	Nourishment of truth.	0 – 1 – 2 – 3 – 4 – 5	
• Incubation:		0 – 1 – 2 – 3 – 4 – 5	
• Education:		0 – 1 – 2 – 3 – 4 – 5	
• Application:		0 – 1 – 2 – 3 – 4 – 5	
• Reproduction:	Reproducing reproducers.		
• Training:		0 – 1 – 2 – 3 – 4 – 5	
• Application:		0 – 1 – 2 – 3 – 4 – 5	
• Sportsmanship:	Encouraging a Christian sports culture.	0 – 1 – 2 – 3 – 4 – 5	

Prayer and Planning: See:' Sports Ministry Events' Planning Suggestions and Checklist
- Core group monthly prayer/planning meeting.
- Inform churches and intercessory team of this initiative.
- Pray daily for the outreach and for those who will attend.
- Pray during church services for the outreach event.
- Target a specific age group and possible handicap level.
- Encourage your sports ministry group to bring their friends and team mates.
- Create an invitation to be presented to friends personally.
  - Make it clear that this includes a dinner and after dinner Christian speaker (when appropriate).
  - Think hard about whether you would accept someone who would not attend the full day.
  - Be disciplined about pre-booking.
- Create a poster to display in sports halls, gyms and churches.
  - See appendix 6 for church poster ideas.
- Find a suitable course that will accept block-bookings.

- Negotiate price: green fee, meals, assembly rooms, prizes.
- Decide on the type of competition, handicap arrangements, team leaders and numbers available.
- Decide on proclamation emphasis: formal/informal.
- Choose an appropriate dinner venue and time. On course site is always recommended if available.

Carry-on and follow-up plans:
- Invite your friends to your church's next guest-service.
- Invite them to a Sports Outreach Discovery Team.
- Plan on another round together in the coming month.

Programme suggestions:
- **Golf outreach**
    - Prepare 'welcomers' to disseminate information and create a friendly atmosphere.
    - Arrange for a registration table at an obvious location.
    - Coffee and roll should be made available.
    - Name tags can help encourage conversation.
    - Keep to starting time and when allowed, a shotgun format (players spread and start at various holes throughout the course) can be helpful for finishing together.
    - After play, hand in cards quickly, tally and display.
- **Meal/presentations:**
    - Create a warm, welcoming, upbeat atmosphere for all the guests.
    - Create a strategic seating plan with a host at each table to facilitate good discussion.
    - Your Master of Ceremonies must be clear and concise and ideally from the community (See Appendix 1).
    - Start the evening with a small introduction.
    - Work with your food preparers and clearly explain your programme.
        - Explain you do not want to be disturbed with clear-up half way through the presentation.
    - Do not cram too much into the programme – less is more! Give ample time for conversation after the meal.
    - Hand out awards and prizes.
    - Prepare your speaker as to the emphasis you want to give to the Christian content, a gentle or full gospel approach.
    - The MC should be prepared to quickly fill in the gaps if any.
    - The guests and speaker should be thanked for coming.
    - Coffee should be served immediately and opportunities for informal discussion should be gently grasped.

Consider closing the meeting with a comment card (see Appendix 4)

Five-a-side Tournament

Planner

Suggestions:

- This could be a big focused opportunity to demonstrate God's love by serving our community with a first-class sports tournament.
- It doesn't have to be soccer.
- Plan on a small epilogue during the awards ceremony.
- Aim at breaking down barriers that the unchurched athletes may have in our community by providing a first-class tournament.
- Your community may be soccer mad so choose to do a soccer tournament this year, and perhaps plan to do a multi-sport competition next year.
- To share Christ with our sports community and give our church members involved in sport an opportunity to bring their friends and team-mates.
- This will be an annual event, we think it would lose its impact if we did it more often.
- It can also serve to highlight Sports Outreach Discovery Teams.
- There is a very real by-product from these events – we want other churches to experience a well-run sports event so they can experience sports ministry first-hand and catch the vision.

Principles determine method:

Sports Outreach Principle Scale	Low emphasis High emphasis
• Proclamation: Verbalisation of truth	
• Formal Proclamation	0 – 1 – 2 – 3 – 4 – 5
• Informal Proclamation	0 – 1 – 2 – 3 – 4 – 5
• Demonstration: Visualization of truth.	0 – 1 – 2 – 3 – 4 – 5
• Maturation: Nourishment of truth.	0 – 1 – 2 – 3 – 4 – 5
• Incubation:	0 – 1 – 2 – 3 – 4 – 5
• Education:	0 – 1 – 2 – 3 – 4 – 5
• Application:	0 – 1 – 2 – 3 – 4 – 5
• Reproduction: Reproducing reproducers.	
• Training:	0 – 1 – 2 – 3 – 4 – 5
• Application:	0 – 1 – 2 – 3 – 4 – 5
• Sportsmanship: Encouraging a Christian sports culture.	0 – 1 – 2 – 3 – 4 – 5

Prayer and planning: See:'Sports Ministry Events' Planning Suggestions and Checklist

- Core group monthly prayer/planning meeting.
- Inform churches and intercessory team of this initiative.
- Pray daily for the outreach and for those that will attend.
- Pray during church service for the outreach event like they would for any other evangelistic campaign.

- Target specific age group or mix: 'Dads & lasses'...
- Encourage your sports ministry group to bring their friends and team-mates.
- Create an invitation to be presented to friends personally.
- Create a quality poster to display in shops, churches, schools and clubs.
  - Make it clear that this includes Christian content when appropriate.
  - Be disciplined about pre-booking.
  - Write up an announcement for the local newspaper.
- Choose a strategic date and time – preferably not during a World Cup final.
- Choose and book a good central venue well in advance.
- Choose your time wisely and stay on track.
- The more help the better.
- Walk your volunteers through the programme well in advance.
- To keep the tournament moving along you will need more than one pitch set up.
  - Three to six is optimal.
- Figure in a budget and entry fee.
  - Purchase trophies and do not skimp on cost.
  - Can you get sponsorship for T-shirts…?
- Choose age groups. Break down the ages as fairly as possible; 11-13 and 14-17 is an average split.

Carry-on and follow-up plans:
- Invite them to a Sports Outreach Discovery Team.
- Special Guest Church Service.
- Invite them to a sports camp or mini camp.

TOURNAMENT SUGGESTIONS:
- Start on time with a brief organizational meeting to explain where everything is, specific rules, times and competitions.
- Give armbands to designated captains who will disseminate further information.
- Start your competitions on time and keep the games moving.
- Think of some alternative sports, coaching or activities that can be played along side the tournament like: music, BBQ., Bouncy Boxing, sub-tournament on computer games, video highlights of their match....
- Awards and Epilogue:
  - This is can be as low-key or as extravagant as you have the time, means, speaker and skills. Again plan well in advance and choose what tempo you want to strive for in your outreach.
  - Hand out awards. You can show brief clips of the evening's highlights on video if you have the equipment.
  - Speaker with relevant sports-related message.
  - Hand out Christian sporty tracts
  - Having a Sports Church Service the next week can be a natural bridge from the community to church.

Iron-man Night

Planner

Suggestions:

- This is our fun opportunity to spend focused time with a relatively small group. Hire a gymnasium or school sports hall for the night, set up a marathon of games and competitions, and stay up all night. Plan on a small epilogue during the evening and watch a movie.
- Aim at breaking down barriers that the unchurched athletes may have in our community by providing a crazy evening of fun events.
- To share Christ with your sports community and give your church members involved in sport an opportunity to bring their friends and team-mates.
- This could be an annual event with very little set up.
- It will also serve to highlight a Sports Outreach Discovery Team.
- One of the best by-products of this event are the relationships that are built.

Principles determine method:

Sports Outreach Principle Scale	Low emphasis High emphasis
• Proclamation: Verbalisation of truth.	
• Formal Proclamation	0 – 1 – 2 – 3 – 4 – 5
• Informal Proclamation	0 – 1 – 2 – 3 – 4 – 5
• Demonstration: Visualization of truth.	0 – 1 – 2 – 3 – 4 – 5
• Maturation: Nourishment of truth.	0 – 1 – 2 – 3 – 4 – 5
• Incubation:	0 – 1 – 2 – 3 – 4 – 5
• Education:	0 – 1 – 2 – 3 – 4 – 5
• Application:	0 – 1 – 2 – 3 – 4 – 5
• Reproduction: Reproducing reproducers.	
• Training:	0 – 1 – 2 – 3 – 4 – 5
• Application:	0 – 1 – 2 – 3 – 4 – 5
• Sportsmanship: Encouraging a Christian sports culture.	0 – 1 – 2 – 3 – 4 – 5

Prayer and planning: See: 'Sports Ministry Events' Planning Suggestions and Checklist

- Core group monthly prayer/ planning meeting.
- Inform churches and intercessory team of this initiative.
- Pray daily for the outreach and for those who will attend.
- Pray during church services for the outreach event like they would for any other evangelistic campaign.
- Target specific age group.
- Encourage your sports ministry group to bring their friends and team-mates.
- Create an invitation to be presented to friends personally.
- Create a quality poster to display in shops, churches, schools and clubs.

- Make it clear that this includes Christian content when appropriate.
- Be disciplined about pre-booking.
- Choose and book a good central venue well in advance.
- Choose your time wisely and stay on track.
- The more help the better.

Carry-on and follow-up plans:
- Invite them to a Sports Outreach Discovery Team.
- Invite them to a sports camp or mini-camp.
- Having a Sports Church Service the next week can be a natural bridge from the pitch to the church.

SUGGESTIONS:
- Enter all the groups into teams and try to make them as fair as possible.
- Create a marathon of games, sports quizzes and competitions.
- Have a couple of sports videos to break it up.
- Order pizzas or fish and chips.
- Have a speaker, more games.
- Quick breakfast and home after six.
- Encourage them to bring sleeping bags and offer opportunities to sleep.
- Music, Bouncy Boxing, sub-tournament on computer games, Video highlights of their competitions....
- Create awards for best team, Sportsman of the night for best sportsmanship....
    - Hand out Christian sporty tracts.
    - Having a Sports Church Service the next week can be a natural bridge from the gymnasium to the church.

Match Day

Planner
Suggestions
- To infuse the excitement and aura of a sporting event (professional match) with a sports ministry event.
- To incorporate a Christian sporty road show with a professional football match.
- Provide an easy avenue of invitation to unchurched friends.
- Create an opportunity to clearly hear a formal proclamation of the gospel.
- Furnish scope for friendship and informal proclamation.
- Reach a clientele (of all ages) traditionally outside the church (sporty people).
- This could be an annual event to help build momentum for your sports ministry.

Principles determine method:

Sports Outreach Principle Scale	Low emphasis	High emphasis
• Proclamation: Verbalisation of truth		
• Formal Proclamation	0 – 1 – 2 – 3 – 4 – 5	
• Informal Proclamation	0 – 1 – 2 – 3 – 4 – 5	
• Demonstration: Visualization of truth.	0 – 1 – 2 – 3 – 4 – 5	
• Maturation: Nourishment of truth.	0 – 1 – 2 – 3 – 4 – 5	
• Incubation:	0 – 1 – 2 – 3 – 4 – 5	
• Education:	0 – 1 – 2 – 3 – 4 – 5	
• Application:	0 – 1 – 2 – 3 – 4 – 5	
• Reproduction: Reproducing reproducers.		
• Training:	0 – 1 – 2 – 3 – 4 – 5	
• Application:	0 – 1 – 2 – 3 – 4 – 5	
• Sportsmanship: Encouraging a Christian sports culture.	0 – 1 – 2 – 3 – 4 – 5	

Prayer and planning: See: 'Sports Ministry Events' Planning Suggestions and Checklist
- Core group monthly prayer/planning meeting.
- Inform churches and intercessory team of this initiative.
- Pray daily for the outreach and for those that will attend.
- Pray during church services for the outreach event like they would for any other evangelistic campaign.
- This is a brilliant opportunity to invite everyone who loves sport.
- Encourage your sports ministry group to bring their friends and team-mates.
- Create an invitation to be presented to friends personally.
- Create a quality poster to display in shops, churches, schools and clubs.
  - Make it clear that this includes Christian content when appropriate.
  - Be disciplined about pre-booking.
- Write up an announcement for the local newspaper.

SPORTS OUTREACH

Carry-on and Follow-up plans:

- This is an easy way to invite your sports-mad neighbour who is outside the church fellowship. It creates a brilliant time for informal conversations about Christ after hearing a clear proclamation of the gospel. It is a long memorable day to build relationships and create openness to the gospel. It is also something for the whole family.
    - Your best 'next step' may be inviting them to a special guest service at your church.
    - Invite them to a sports camp or mini-camp.
    - Invite them to a Sports Outreach Discovery Team.

Warnings:

- Though Match Day is geared around sport it can lend itself to the sports fan as well as the sportsperson. This is great but in follow-up be sensitive where you invite them. Sports Outreach Teams are tailored for athletes not for the casual sports fan. 'I have become all things to all men so that by all possible means I might save some' (1 Cor. 9:22).
- Be careful which match you see. Some venues may not be suitable for bringing Christian groups. If you can sit together it creates a better atmosphere.

Programme: Match-Day/ Road-Show suggested itinerary: (See 'Sports Ministry Events' Planning Suggestions and Checklist)

- Registration & welcome team
    - Encourage groups to come in teams of five or six – arrange and combine groups that arrive without a team.
- Enter into sports hall to music, sports video or live music
- Intro from 'Master of Ceremonies'. This job is crucial in setting the tone and pace of the road show. Not all are gifted at this, get the right person in place (See appendix 1).
- Competition: Javelin throw, one person per team, foam javelin or ball (into goal)
- Wide screen video quiz
- Music (live) or sports video?
- Competition: basketball shoot
- Video testimony or live interview
- Competition: press-ups and 'Pit Spray award!'
- Music: band
- Speaker
- Awards and rap (someone to promote camp)
- Food and live music
- Walk or drive to stadium

CHECKLIST:
- MC and speaker: (See appendix 1)
- Awards, hats, Sports Bibles, pit spray (always a fun award!)
- Sports literature: tracts or a Christian sports magazine
- Wide screen video projector
- Competition equipment: Football net, BB net, balls, video quiz, golf chip…
- Local sportsperson for testimony?
- PA system
- Food
- Live music
- Banners, leaflets and camera
- Venue: Sports hall or gymnasium, preferably in immediate location to the game
- Interactive games
- Live music
- Music videos
- Local sporty testimonies
- Fun prizes
- Speaker
- Food and refreshments
- Attend match together
- Pre-train folks to share their faith

SPORTS OUTREACH

Night of Champions

Planner

Purpose: Night of Champions is an outdoor competition (or indoor) with an indoor Christian sporty road-show. It combines the opportunity to engage in sport and the entertainment of a sports night.

- To share Christ with our sports community and give our church members involved in sport an opportunity to bring their friends and team-mates.
- There are several by-products of a N O C including:
- Exposure to sports ministry to churches and create a desire for long-term ministry.
  - It can identify and help train potential leaders.
  - It can be an annual event
  - It can serve as a channel to people to the Sports Impact Discovery Course.

Principles determine method:
Sports Outreach Principle Scale.

		Low emphasis	High emphasis
• Proclamation:	Verbalisation of truth		
• Formal Proclamation		0 – 1 – 2 – 3 – 4 – 5	
• Informal Proclamation		0 – 1 – 2 – 3 – 4 – 5	
• Demonstration:	Visualization of truth.	0 – 1 – 2 – 3 – 4 – 5	
• Maturation:	Nourishment of truth.	0 – 1 – 2 – 3 – 4 – 5	
• Incubation:		0 – 1 – 2 – 3 – 4 – 5	
• Education:		0 – 1 – 2 – 3 – 4 – 5	
• Application:		0 – 1 – 2 – 3 – 4 – 5	
• Reproduction:	Reproducing reproducers.		
• Training:		0 – 1 – 2 – 3 – 4 – 5	
• Application:		0 – 1 – 2 – 3 – 4 – 5	
• Sportsmanship:	Encouraging a Christian sports culture.	0 – 1 – 2 – 3 – 4 – 5	

Prayer and planning: See:'Sports Ministry Events' Planning Suggestions and Checklist

- Core group monthly prayer/planning meeting.
- Inform churches and intercessory team of this initiative.
- Pray daily for the outreach and for those that will attend.
- Pray during church services for the outreach event as they would for any other evangelistic campaign.
- Target a specific age group.
- Encourage your sports ministry group to bring their friends and team-mates.
- Create an invitation to be presented to friends personally.
- Create a quality poster to display in shops, churches, schools and clubs.
  - Make it clear that this includes Christian content when appropriate.
  - Be disciplined about pre-booking.

- Write up an announcement for the local newspaper.
- Encourage sports ministry group to bring two friends
- Create an invitation to be hand delivered to friends and team-mates.
- Write up an announcement for the local newspaper.

Carry-on and follow-up plans:
- Invite them to a Sports Outreach Discovery Course.
- Invite them to a sports camp or mini-camp.
- Having a Sports Church Service the next week can be a natural bridge from the community to church.

Suggested helpers:
- Night of Champions co-ordinator.
- Master Score Keeper
- Game Station Leaders
- Road Show coordinator

Programme:
SUGGESTED Order of events: **Night of Champions:**
Competitions: see appendix 3 for suggested games:
- 30 min – Pre-train 'Games-station leaders'
- 30 min – Registration – encourage advance bookings of teams,
- 60 – 90 min – Intro and games competition
- 15 min – Break, snack, entertainment
- 60 – 90 minutes – Sporty Road Show

Road Show Itinerary:
- Come in to music video sport action clips dubbed with music (youth sit on floor in teams)
- Welcome
- Quick 'Question of Sport' Quiz
- Interview – local sportsperson.
- Music video
- Drama?
- Video sports quiz!
- Press-up competition (pit spray prize!!!)
- Music
- Football Video
- Talk 25 minutes max.
- Awards (base ball hats and Bibles) –
- Hand out comment cards.

SPORTS OUTREACH

Outreach Banquet

Planner

Purpose:

- A special emphasis on sharing Christ with a formal proclamation of the gospel in a non-threatening environment.
- This could be another annual event to add to your Sports Outreach diary.
- This is also a good opportunity to develop a working relationship with other churches in your community.
- Remind your Christian community that this is an evangelistic dinner and at least half should be unchurched.

Principles determine method:

Sports Outreach Principle Scale	Low emphasis High emphasis
• Proclamation: Verbalisation of truth	
• Formal Proclamation	$0-1-2-3-4-5$
• Informal Proclamation	$0-1-2-3-4-5$
• Demonstration: Visualization of truth.	$0-1-2-3-4-5$
• Maturation: Nourishment of truth.	$0-1-2-3-4-5$
• Incubation:	$0-1-2-3-4-5$
• Education:	$0-1-2-3-4-5$
• Application:	$0-1-2-3-4-5$
• Reproduction: Reproducing reproducers.	
• Training:	$0-1-2-3-4-5$
• Application:	$0-1-2-3-4-5$
• Sportsmanship: Encouraging a Christian sports culture	$0-1-2-3-4-5$

Prayer and planning: See:' Sports Ministry Events' Planning Suggestions and Checklist

- Core group monthly prayer/ planning meeting.
- Inform churches and intercessory team of this initiative.
- Pray daily for the outreach and for those that will attend.
- Pray during church services for the outreach event like they would for any other evangelistic campaign.
- Target specific age group and possible skill level.
- Encourage your sports ministry group to bring their friends and team mates.
- Create an invitation to be presented to friends personally.
- Create a quality poster to display in shops, churches, schools and clubs.
  - Make it clear that this includes Christian content when appropriate.
  - Be disciplined about pre-booking.
- Write up an announcement for the local newspaper. This, of all the events modelled here, is one where obtaining a speaker must be well thought through. It would be great to have a famous athlete come and grace your evening. There is a buzz when

an athlete is in the room and it goes a long way in attracting a crowd. But there are few to go around and fewer that can put the gospel across clearly. If you do manage to get a famous speaker who will you get the next year? Sometimes groups use a speaker who is not a person of faith and the whole evening is compromised. What if your famous guest cancels on you? Then who do you get? Is it the job of the famous speaker to attract the crowd for you? Let me suggest that you may have a larger crowd but your long-term objectives may not be achieved. The core of sports ministry is building relationships with other like-minded people. It is those relationships that draw and sustain ministry (See appendix 1).

- An appropriate venue is as important as the speaker. Ask yourself – if I were not a Christian would I want to go to that event?
    - Prep acoustics and don't spread the table out too far, a warm close feel is better.

Carry-on and follow-up plans:

- Invite them to a Sports Outreach Discovery Team.
- Having a Sports Church Service the next week can be a natural bridge from the community to church.

- Programme:
    - Create a warm, welcoming, up beat atmosphere for all the guests.
    - Create a strategic seating plan with host at each table to facilitate good discussion.
    - Your Master of Ceremonies must be clear and concise – it is best if they are from the community.
    - Start the evening with a small introduction.
    - Work with your food preparers and clearly explain your programme.
        - Explain you do not want to be disturbed with clear-up halfway through the presentation.
    - Do not cram too much into the programme – less is more! It is better than running so late they have no time and feel rushed.
    - Video clips and music are helpful and can create a sporty feel.
    - Your speaker should be prepared to give a clear gospel message, and appreciate the fact they are addressing people in the world of sport.
    - The MC should be prepared to quickly fill in the gaps, if any (See Appendix 1).
    - The guest and speaker should be thanked for coming.
    - Coffee should be served immediately and opportunities for informal discussion should be gently grasped.
    - Consider closing the meeting with comment cards (See appendix 4).

SPORTS OUTREACH

Service Project

Planner

Question: What is the first thing a new University Graduate says to you these days?
Answer: Do you want large fries with that Big Mac?

We live in a society where we can feel unwanted and unneeded. It is quite hard for Christian groups to compete in the multi-billion-dollar entertainment business. But we have an opportunity to give people something that they desire: purpose. A service project is a great alternative to the conventional types of sports outreach events. They expose sports people to the realities of poverty, the marginalized and infirmed, and also help them realise the joy and impact they can make by being a servant.

Principles determine method:

Sports Outreach Principle Scale	Low emphasis	High emphasis
• Proclamation: Verbalisation of truth		
• Formal Proclamation	0 – 1 – 2 – 3 – 4 – 5	
• Informal Proclamation	0 – 1 – 2 – 3 – 4 – 5	
• Demonstration: Visualization of truth.	0 – 1 – 2 – 3 – 4 – 5	
• Maturation: Nourishment of truth.	0 – 1 – 2 – 3 – 4 – 5	
• Incubation:	0 – 1 – 2 – 3 – 4 – 5	
• Education:	0 – 1 – 2 – 3 – 4 – 5	
• Application:	0 – 1 – 2 – 3 – 4 – 5	
• Reproduction: Reproducing reproducers.		
• Training:	0 – 1 – 2 – 3 – 4 – 5	
• Application:	0 – 1 – 2 – 3 – 4 – 5	
• Sportsmanship: Encouraging a Christian sports culture.	0 – 1 – 2 – 3 – 4 – 5	

Prayer and Planning: See:' Sports Ministry Events' Planning Suggestions and Checklist

- Core group monthly prayer/planning meeting.
- Inform churches and intercessory team of this initiative.
- Pray daily for the outreach and for those that will attend.
- Pray during church service for the outreach event.
- Encourage your sports ministry group to bring their friends and team mates.
- Create an invitation to be presented to friends personally.
- Create a poster to display in sports – halls, gyms and churches.
  - Be disciplined about pre-booking.
- This particular outreach usually needs no specific age group target.
- Introduce Sports Outreach Discovery Teams

Carry-on and follow-up plans:
- Invite them to a Sports Impact Discovery Course.
- Invite them to a sports camp or mini-camp.
- Having a Sports Church Service the next week can be a natural bridge from the community to church.

Programme: People rarely get opportunities to serve; this can be a great time for your group to feel valued and to give of themselves.
- Possibly give a sports demonstration at an old folks home!
- Do an assembly at a nursery or day care.
- Give training tips to young kids at the primary school.
- Take your group to volunteer at a city mission.
- Raise money for specific mission agencies like Tear Fund.
- Challenge the Christian members of your group to give a two-minute testimony and spend some time training them! Stretch them.

SPORTS OUTREACH

Christian Teams and Church Sports Leagues

Christian teams and Church sports' leagues have been in operation for many years. I have met several Christians who were introduced to the gospel through a Church Sports League. Most leagues exist to create opportunities for 'outreach' and to influence the community. They also provide church athletes with a healthy environment for competition (in theory) and to practise putting their faith in action. Leagues can unify churches and create an attractive environment for the unchurched.

Benefits:
- Opportunities for church members to serve the body of Christ.
- Accomplishing outreach through non-traditional yet relevant means.
- Cross-denominational fellowship among churches.
- Inroads into the sports community.
- Involvement of church members who love sport.
- Disciplining and building better athletes.
- Environment for healthy competition.
- Modelling Biblical principles in a social setting.

Suggested goals:
- Opportunities to develop new relationships.
- Strengthening relationships between believers.
- Impact the local community, city, or national sport programmes.
- Provide contact opportunities for participants.
- Provide participants with a well-organized league.
- To do outreach through non-traditional yet relevant means.

Survey for spiritual health of your Church league:
- Church leagues have been a great success all around the world, but for every good example of a 'Church League' we find another which has lost its purpose. Sports Outreach has been asked on several occasions to evaluate local church leagues and give workable ideas on how to make them better, to refocus and help them function with purpose.

- The first four questions we ask cure 90 per cent of Church Leagues' problems:
    - Are the Christians in the league getting together and praying for the un-churched in the league?
    - Are your churches praying for your league?
    - Are you training your Christians to share the gospel with those participating in the league who are 'outside the church'?
    - Are your core leaders committed to your core values?

SPORTS OUTREACH

Vision for sports leagues:
- To bring together churches of various denominations within a community. To build relationships and proclaim the good news of Jesus Christ in a non-threatening manner.
- A sports league can provide quality competition, fellowship, and promote the unifying love of Christ and Biblical values that develop spiritual characteristics within sport persons.

 Suggested ingredients for your sports ministry:

- *A place that proclaims truth*
- *A tool for discipleship*
- *A means of fellowship*
- *A source of support*
- *A teacher of servanthood*
- *A trainer of leaders*
- *A healthy environment*

SPORTS OUTREACH

Sports Camps and Mini - Camps

Planner

Purpose:

- To build meaningful relationships while away from the everyday stresses of life (See Appendix 5).
- To create an atmosphere where the gospel can be proclaimed in a relevant manner.
- To provide an enjoyable opportunity for coaching and competition.
- To give an opportunity to experience what a week's sports camp could be like.

Principles determine method:

Sports Outreach Principle Scale	Low emphasis High emphasis
• Proclamation: Verbalisation of truth	
• Formal Proclamation	0 – 1 – 2 – 3 – 4 – 5
• Informal Proclamation	0 – 1 – 2 – 3 – 4 – 5
• Demonstration: Visualization of truth.	0 – 1 – 2 – 3 – 4 – 5
• Maturation: Nourishment of truth.	0 – 1 – 2 – 3 – 4 – 5
• Incubation:	0 – 1 – 2 – 3 – 4 – 5
• Education:	0 – 1 – 2 – 3 – 4 – 5
• Application:	0 – 1 – 2 – 3 – 4 – 5
• Reproduction: Reproducing reproducers.	
• Training:	0 – 1 – 2 – 3 – 4 – 5
• Application:	0 – 1 – 2 – 3 – 4 – 5
• Sportsmanship: Encouraging a Christian sports culture.	0 – 1 – 2 – 3 – 4 – 5

Prayer and planning times: See:'Sports Ministry Events' Planning Suggestions and Checklist
- Core group prayer and lead-up time.
- Inform our church's intercessory team of this initiative.
- Pray daily for the outreach and for those who will attend.
- Pray during church services for the outreach event.
- Encourage your sports ministry group to bring their friends and team-mates.
- Create an invitation to be personally given out.

Consider:

- Decide on whether you want to have a multi-sport camp or mini-camp or stick to one main sport.
- Target your age group and possible skill level.
- Provide opportunities for competition, instruction and possibly fun games.
- Develop basic skills.
- Provide for advanced skill training.
- Individual and team strategy.

- Video instruction and/or review (replay drills or competition).
- Personal evaluation and fitness programmes.
- Could this be done at a local or national level.
- Choose a location that will have access to proper sporting facilities.
- Plan your time line.
- Plan a budget.
- How many leaders and coaches will we need?
  - I suggest no more than a 1 leader to 6 athletes ratio.
- Create a check list (See appendix 5 for ideas).

Carry-on and follow-up plans:
- Invite participants to guest sports service.
- Invite them to a Sports Outreach Discovery Team.

Programme suggestions:

Friday:
Welcome, registration, bank, assign teams
Bus leaves for venue.
Team photo
Warm-up, coaching and competitions
Dinner
Free time
Warm-up & team challenge
Evening team meeting
Small group meeting
Lights out

Saturday:
On the green with the Dean (Optional)
Power time: *warm-up, minute-message, focus-time*
Breakfast
Morning team meeting
Morning training session
Lunch
Afternoon training session
Option time
Free time
Dinner
Team challenge
Evening team meeting
Travel home

SPORTS OUTREACH

School Sports Mission Teams

The culture of sport and education are very diverse from one country to another. There are many pros and cons of the separation of church and state. My guess is that this section on a school mission will not resonate with many North American groups where Christian groups are rarely allowed the access that some European countries have. Nevertheless this programme can be adapted to a variety of settings. If your group or organisation is invited to do a school mission it will offer you a real catalyst to start or expand ongoing work. They provide support and credibility to the Christians at the school and provide a higher profile for Christian input.

What a school sports mission team can offer,which is different from other significant and valuable mission organizations is **sport.** Sport brings the great advantage of being able to break down barriers very quickly with boys and girls in schools. Not only does the sports mission team lead assemblies and work in classroom situations, where they can talk about being a Christian and answer questions, but it also goes in and teaches football, cricket, hockey and netball and works within the games and PE contexts.

By speaking the universal language of sport the right has been earned, much more quickly than without that language, to be able to relate easily and to share the gospel of Jesus in a relevant way within that particular social context.

Pre-mission

Recruiting – get a team which can participate in the sports, particularly the ones offered that term. Pray that the sports mission team will have an environment where they will clearly share the gospel. A pre-mission visit is helpful to see the facilities and identify the objectives of the school (usually you will be invited by the head of religious studies, chaplain or a sympathetic administrator). Plan a post-mission follow-up.

Assemblies

School assemblies can be very helpful in establishing a profile for the week. The mission team has an opportunity for a large audience to see what they have been hearing about in pre-mission publicity. Assemblies can set the tone and tempo for the mission. Assemblies can introduce a Christian message in a relevant manner, which may be completely new to the students.

The window of opportunity in an assembly is very short. After settling the pupils and giving announcements, most schools will allow about 5–1 0 minutes, so communication has to be succinct and to the point. It is easy to err either way – coming on too strong trying to convert the entire school in 7 quick minutes or being so covert, that the students never identify you with Christ at all.

Balance is the key to any school assembly. Be organized, enthusiastic and know what you want to communicate.

Classroom preparation

Prayer is the best preparation, know your material thoroughly and have examples ready. If you have more than one day of classes, plan variety and build a theme into your lessons.

Attitude

- Work with and serve the teacher, whose class you are taking. You are a guest and the teacher could use your support.
- When doing a presentation in class take control.
- Do not be afraid of the class.
- Love the class with God's love.

General techniques

- Face the class at all times, do not speak into the blackboard.
- Have a calm, clear voice that can be heard throughout the entire classroom.
- Create a sense of expectancy in the class. Keep the students guessing what you are going to do next.
- Involve the whole class and allow them to ask questions. Be prepared to say, 'I don't know, I will try to find-out'.
- Involve several of your team members.
- Think through discipline and carry it out consistently and fairly when appropriate.

Physical education

- PE is a great opportunity for you to serve. You have an expertise in sport that is a gift from God. The pupils may not understand or appreciate your attempts to share Christ with them, they may even resent it, but they will not resent you offering your sporting expertise. This can be a valuable means of showing that you actually care for them personally and not just as another punter to be notched on your Bible.
- Be organized.
- Serve the PE teacher.
- Give an opportunity for questions and answers.

Assembly example

Bring in a uniform of your sport: hockey goalie kit, cricket batsman kit or even American Football gear. Ask for one volunteer – choose someone small but with pluck. Have them put on the kit and teach them one silly sports technique like how to block a shot or a three-point stance. Explain that sports people can build their lives around one of three things : possessions, performance or appearance.

Possibly get members of the mission team to explain one concept each. Professional sportsmen build their lives on possessions – fast cars… appearance – right hair cut, reputation… performance: – (I was once told) 'you will only be around until someone comes that is a little faster than you, stronger than you or cheaper than you then you are gone!' Then explain that the problem with performance, possessions and appearance is that they do not last.

'There once was a religious man named Sam, who was told by God he had to find a king for the Jewish nation. Sam looked all over for a suitable king. He looked for a man of great wealth and God said, "no". He looked for a man that possessed great talent as a hunter and God said "no". He looked for a man who was tall and strong and God said, "no". Based (loosely) on 1 Samuel 16:7, God says "Man looks at the outside of a man but I (God) look at the heart".'

After-school training
- Be disciplined.
- Support the coach.
- If you get an opportunity to travel to an away match, take it! That can be a brilliant way to build relationships.

Evening meetings
- Music
- Tickets to sell and give away
- Drama
- Interviews
- Involve Christian students and staff
- Keep to time
- Build and stick to a theme
- Fun games
- Multimedia

Appendix 1

The Good Christian Guide: On How to Treat a Speaker

- When securing a speaker give them a clear idea of your aims and objectives for the talk.
- Pray for your speaker prior to event.
- Be clear and forthright with expenses and speaking fees.
- Find out about what they do: can you give them an opportunity to talk about their ministry?
- Provide a clear detailed map.
- Provide a contact person and emergency phone number.
- Provide a venue phone number.
- Suggest appropriate attire. (I have often arrived at an event after the contact person said, 'you wear what is comfortable, no problem' only to find myself the only one there in casual clothes and feeling a bit awkward.)
- Offer accommodation/meals. But also understand they may rather shoot off home than feel obliged to spend time with a family they will never meet again – give them the option.
- Provide chaperone/attendant for your speaker as a buffer against cranks that want to brag about their sporting prowess. Instead maximise their time by introducing them to people that may earnestly want to speak with them.
- Provide clear objectives for the meeting (evangelistic, pastoral, instructional, motivational... do not say 'all of the above'!).
- Describe the audience (kids? adults? Women's Institute?)
- Is there a theme?
- Give the speaker a time and time limits.
- Provide an itinerary, order of service (before a meal, after a song...?)
- Provide prayer for speaker before or after talk.
- Welcome the speaker and make them feel comfortable.
- Don't smother the speaker, give them opportunity to gather their thoughts.

Choose your Master of Ceremonies wisely; this is not a default position. The MC will set the tempo and atmosphere for the evening and can either make or break a good event.

- The Master of Ceremonies is the link from one stage of the proceedings to the next.
- The MC may also interview others in the programme who don't feel comfortable speaking on their own. Help them prepare.
- They are also often the best host of the visiting speaker.
- It is important that the MC has the following qualities:

SPORTS OUTREACH

- Ability to see what is going on and to sense the mood of the event.
- Good example of a Christian man/woman with wisdom and experience.
- Skilled at delegating.
- Able to make the speaker and guests feel welcome and at ease.
- Reasonably good at public speaking and prepared to be impromptu when necessary.
- Feel comfortable opening in prayer.
- Give out notices and keep the event moving on schedule.
- Welcome everyone.
- Talk to the speaker during the meal – be a servant.
    - Does the speaker need anything?
    - Ensure he knows how long to speak for.
    - Whether the speaker will take questions...
- Introduce speaker. Please be enthusiastic and research the speaker beforehand.
- Thank speaker and guests.
- Bid farewell to leaving guests.
- Contact the speaker afterwards.
    - I have found that an encouraging phonecall on the drive home or the next day in the office has been warmly appreciated.

Create a good atmosphere in the venue for your guests and speaker:
- Proper lighting.
- Room set-up, (file audience into front of venue NOT back of venue).
- Appropriate music.
- Prepare your food servers: help them understand when and when not to clear up, serve coffee...
- Proper sound system.
    - In the event of a power cut and you have 3000 at the venue how do you get your speaker heard? Plan ahead – hire a generator.
- Overhead Projectors?
- Appropriate size of venue: a smaller room full is a better atmosphere than a big auditorium with guests dotted around the back of the hall.

(Example letter to speaker)

Sports Outreach
Quiz & Curry Night

Dear

Thank you for agreeing to come to our Sports Outreach: Quiz & Curry Night. We have a great night planned and look forward to hearing 'Your Story'.

Beginning in January _____ we intend to run a series called, 'My Story'. The purpose of this series is to invite Christians in various sports to come and tell their story which we will programme into one of our Sports Outreach Events: We will be holding three of these nights throughout the year:

- January: Quiz & Curry
- May: Night of Champions
- November: Coaching Clinic

We would like you to speak during the 'My Story' segment of the Q & C Night. 'My Story' is the segment of our programme when we invite an outside guest to explain how Christ is relevant in their lives and to unpack the gospel in relation to their experience. We would like you to bring a Scripture reading that is important to you and speak for 20-30 minutes. At the end of this time it would be our intention to open up the meeting to take questions from the floor. We are planning to run an eight week Sports Impact Discovery Team that will correspond with this event.

Publicity

It would be our intention to view these meetings as 'formal proclamation' opportunities. We would intend inviting people we have made contact with from our various sporting contacts built up in the communities. We will attempt to gain some press coverage for this series, to create an exposure to the concept of Christians in sport. Accordingly we may want to take a few photographs to assist with getting press coverage.

Pen Portrait

In order to make sure that we get your details correct for any publicity or press interest, I would be grateful if you could supply in the **space below** a brief description of who you are, what you do and what your interests are, then e-mail it back to me.

When and Where

The date we talked about was the __ Jan__. The quiz night will start at 7.30pm and we would be grateful if you could arrange to arrive at 7.00 pm. The venue is:_____. And detailed directions are supplied on next page.

Further Information
Call _____on _____ or e-mail _____
Mobile _____
Venue Number:_____

SPORTS OUTREACH

 Appendix 2

Church Prospectus
A Model Proposal for Your Church

In this proposal, we hope to introduce you to the idea of sports evangelism and discipleship in the context of the local church. This is not an exhaustive paper but we hope it will whet your appetite and enable you to get started in your own situation.

The Church has always had a rather ambivalent attitude to sport. While several league football clubs have their origins in churches, the view has tended to develop in churches throughout the twentieth century that sport is worldly and not something that devoted Christians should be involved in. Furthermore, the fact that sport is sometimes played on Sundays lends credence to the view that sport should be viewed with suspicion.

On the other hand, sport is increasingly being seen as a vehicle to reach young people and bring adults within the natural orbit of the Christian community.

It is our contention that sport can be a vital part of our church programme, coming along-side the youth ministry, music minstry, women's ministry, etc. 'Sports Ministry' often crosses all aspects of the church community. There is certainly nothing wrong with enjoying sport, As Eric Liddle says in *Chariots Of Fire*, 'God made me for a purpose but he also made me fast and when I run I feel his pleasure.' Increasingly Christians have come to see sport, played with the right attitude, as something that can bring pleasure to God.

However, the motivation in any local church sports programme must be outreach. Too often evangelism has only happened in set-up situations – the guest service, big crusades, street preaching, etc. By using sport, we can build relationships and create situations in which we can talk to people about Jesus as naturally as possible in a relaxed atmosphere.

Research (such as 'Finding Faith Today – how does it happen?') suggests that most people from non-church backgrounds attribute their conversion to Christianity to the influence of a Christian friend. Sport provides an excellent way of making friends which can be developed into an evangelistic opportunity.

SPORTS OUTREACH

Sports Outreach:
Formation Letter for your Church

Purpose:

- To build a healthy, non-threatening 'port-of-entry' for both our church and sports community.
- To provide the framework of training and encouragement for athletes already involved in the Church. To teach Christian values, build Christian character, and develop specific skills in the sports and recreation area.
- To demonstrate that our worship extends to the ways in which we play and enjoy our sports and recreational activities.
- To provide a focused outreach to the athletes and coaches who live and work in our area.

Why a Sports Outreach ministry for our church?

- *Note: please call your sports ministry whatever your faith community sees fit, I use Sports Outreach for the harmony of this book, it is merely a simple and clear title. We are interested in reaching the sports world for Christ not in building a big para-organisation.*

As individuals and as a church we are all called to go into all the world, to 'become all things to all men that by all means that (we) might save some.' We are also called to help our brother and sister grow in their faith, as well as to encourage each other. All of these things are possible through involvement in a sports programme committed to using sport and recreation as a vehicle to reach, disciple and to encourage. Sport and recreation offer a unique opportunity to 'let (our) light shine before men,' to draw, strengthen, and develop leadership. This cohesive ministry concept is pivotal to all our initiatives.

The quality and diversity of our Sports Outreach ministry is directly proportionate to the number of people called by God to serve in our church. If you can coach, referee or help with organization, ask God to show you direct avenues of ministry. If you feel you have been gifted by God to serve in this area pray God will open the door for you to serve through sport in this church.

BENEFITS of a Sports Outreach ministry in our church:

Opportunities:
- To reach the unchurched.
- To engage in positive and constructive leisure activity.

- To apply Christian principles and create a Christian culture in play, competition and sports.
- For social interaction and physical exercise.
- For creating an atmosphere to strengthen the family life.
- Opportunity to better make new contacts and establish new friends.

Sports ministry also:
- Provides a natural atmosphere to mentor youth.
- Cultivates spiritual growth and leadership among believers.
- Develops interest and skills leading to lifelong enjoyment.
- Provides a tool for Christian education and missions action.
- Provides a ministry 'Beyond the Sanctuary – To Play Away'
- Creates a holistic individual.
- Offers a place of service and support among sporty lay-people.
- Breaks down social barriers and builds stronger Christ-centred relationships.
- Supports the family unit, through positive leisure opportunities.
- Provides release from tension and stress caused in today's hurried-up society.

Sportsmanship in our church:

Reflecting Christ is our aim:
Our Sports Outreach ministry is an integral part of the total ministry of the church and should not seen as separate. Our programmes should be seen as an incubator for living and developing Christian growth. Yet, we must be aware that good sportsmanship is not an automatic response and should be encouraged and cultivated. The dangers of putting sport ahead of God are real. To God sin is sin: unsportsman-like behaviour is as ungodly as if you were to scream obscenities in Church. Many important and positive values can be learned from competition. But there are several ungodly characteristics, which Christians seem to turn a blind eye to on the pitch. It is no wonder there are struggles with resisting church leaders, who have seen their church attempt a football match which turned into a riot. Imagine what signals an undisciplined, self-indulgent church team sends to its community.

Building leaders:
As in all programmes of our church, leadership has an important place in the sports ministry. Because of the potential for constructive or destructive behaviour, we must seek to find and develop the best possible Christian leaders for a sports ministry programme. The spiritual qualifications must be as, if not more important than athletic ability, leadership skills or other expertise and factors.

Leisure is a gift from God:
It must be remembered that Christ wants us to have and live the 'abundant life'. He wants us to enjoy life, but also to beware of worldly sins. This is even more reason for our church to

SPORTS OUTREACH

provide healthy leisure time and opportunities to impact our community. We must develop within our sports ministry a real sense of good and evil. We must see that there are things in which Christians cannot participate. Our Sports Outreach programme must be geared to training our members in the proper use of leisure: to understand it is a gift from God to be engaged in, enjoyed and used for His glory. We must provide a warm and friendly atmosphere within our fellowship for healthy recreation and keep the integrity of sport at the highest level.

Appendix 3

Night of Champions

Things to do:

Pre-registration & times
Registration & team
Posters, publicity & school visits
Food
Ticket costing
Sales: food, shirts…
Free T-shirts
Budget
Games station
Games station leaders
Venue coordinator
Follow-up (cards)
Follow-up team
Team leaders (team)
Encouragement team
Prayer team
Security team
First aid
Indoor Road Show budget (in house?)
Video projector, MC
PA, lighting, band, local testimony
Prizes
Literature (tracts)
Sunday ecumenical sporty youth service?

GAME STATIONS
Notes: GAME STATION LEADERS:

- This is a sports-oriented activity but the games will not alienate (most) non-sporty kids.
- The competition section is to last one to one-and-a-half hours.
- Most games stations are geared to last about two minutes each.
- Keep a master list - scoring appropriately.
- If your station scores by time: take top five times, scoring ten points for best time, nine for next best time....
- Check off team's score sheet, teams cannot repeat games until all games have been completed once.

SPORTS OUTREACH

- Please take good care of supplies, balls, clubs and string...
- Return supplies to designated spot.
- Return scorecard to Master Score Keeper.
- Hand-outs (hand out literature after road show or through door at end)
- Thanks for all your help!

Station 1: BASKETBALL (3 B-BALLS)
7 to 10 youth shoot one basket each. Score = baskets made.

Station 2: TENNIS JUGGLE (TEN TENNIS BALLS)
Put group in circle (same number of kids every time), pass one ball back & forth, add balls until one is dropped. Score = how many balls in the air.

Station 3: SOCCER (3 S-BALLS)
Goals. . .

Station 4: FRISBEE ACCURACY (FRISBEES AND HOOP)
7 to 10 tries, Score = times through hoop.

Station 5: SUMMO (DUMMIES & STRING CIRCLE, STOP WATCH)
2 youth try to push score keeper out of circle, (for 10 seconds), if any one touches a knee the game is over. Score = draw 5 points, win 10 points, loss 2 points.

Station 6: KEY THROUGH SHIRT (KEY & STRING, STOP WATCH)
Pass key through both sleeves. Score by time.

Station 7: NERF SHOOT (8 NERF GUNS, BUCKET, CONES, STOP WATCH)
One minute to shoot as many arrows into bucket. Score by arrows.

Station 8: CANDLE QUENCH (CANDLE, 4 SQUIRT GUNS, PONCHO, LIGHTER, TIMER)
One member of the team holds candle and wears poncho, while four other members try to quench fire. Score by time

Station 9: VOLLEY PASS (1 VOLLEYBALL)
Keep volley ball in the air, all players must hit the ball, Score by hits per team-mate.

Station 10: BALLOON RELAY (BALLOONS, PLASTIC BAGS, 2 CONES 2 SETS OF UNDERWEAR, TIMER)
Put on underwear, run to 2 relay stations to stuff balloons in underwear, run to finish line, in 1 minute. Score by # of balloons.

Station 11: GOLF CHIP, (2 CLUBS & 12 PLASTIC GOLF BALLS & 1 POT)
Score by balls in pot, in certain time.

Station 12: JAVELIN THROW, (4 FOAM JAVELINS or POOL NOODLES)
Score by distance

Station 13: SHOES (STOP WATCH)
Untangle, Score by time

Station 14: HOCKEY ACCURACY (4 STICKS - 8 BALLS)
How many goals in certain time.

Station 15: BREAK WIND:
The game station leader throws out a balloon and one person has to break, it but they can only use their feet! Score by time.

SPORTS OUTREACH

NIGHT OF CHAMPIONS TEAM SHEET

TEAM#_____

Note:

- Your team must hang on to this sheet and get the Games Station Leaders to tick off Station number after each game.
- Your team must stay together.
- You can not repeat any Station until you have finished all ten Stations.
- The faster you go the more points you will collect.

STATION ROUND 1	STATION ROUND 2
1. _____	1. _____
2. _____	2. _____
3. _____	3. _____
4. _____	4. _____
5. _____	5. _____
6. _____	6. _____
7. _____	7. _____
8. _____	8. _____
9. _____	9. _____
10. _____	10. _____
11. _____	11. _____
12. _____	12. _____
13. _____	13. _____
14. _____	14. _____
15. _____	15. _____

Appendix 4

COMMENT CARD

NAME:_____

ADDRESS:_____ Post Code:_____

_____

Phone #:_____

E-Mail:_____

Please tick the appropriate box:

What did you think of the outdoor sports and games?
[]Great - I loved it   []Fair   []Totally Naff

What did you think of the indoor programme?
[]Totally Cool   []Not Bad   []Keep working on it

Did the main talk make sense to you? []Yes []No

Did you ask Christ into your life tonight? [] Yes []No
[]Not sure

Would you like more information about the Christian faith?
[]Yes   []No

We hold a Sports Outreach Discovery Course (an eight week exploration of Christianity for athletes) Are you interested?

Comments:_____

_____

_____

thanks for coming see you next year

SPORTS OUTREACH

Appendix 5

Camps, Retreats & Missions

A short-term parallel universe

I have heard many leaders tell me: 'My week at a sports camp is the best thing I do all year. The athletes come back enthused and ready to live out their life for Christ, on and off the pitch.' As stated earlier I came to faith through my coach at a Fellowship of Christian Athletes Camp: obviously I believe in sports camps and have helped establish them in several countries. I took a year out recently to develop and co-teach the sports ministry class at Wheaton College, this was as much an education as a time of instruction. I had always enjoyed sports camps and knew they worked, but listening to one of my co-professors Dr Bud Williams, former Chairman of the Board of Christian Camping International, break down the anatomy of a camp was inspiring. His basic premise is that camps, retreats and missions were 'Temporary Systems', a sort of parallel short-term universe. A university, holiday (vacation), retreat, prison and conference were all forms of temporary systems. For that matter a competition is a temporary system, the word 'camp' means temporary dwelling. When we go to a sports camp, retreat, or mission, with others and it is organized with a specific purpose in mind, we are entering a temporary system designed for growth and change. There are special dynamics embedded in that temporary system experience that renders it a powerful tool through which lives are changed.

It is fun! Dr Williams writes, 'Sport is fun and helps us understand a part of the nature of God - that of creative activity for the pure joy of it. God did not have to create our world with beauty, delight and refreshment. But he did and pronounced it good.' Getting away is recreation to recreate. Dr Greg Linville, Professor of Sports Ministry at Malone College, writes, 'Plato once said that, 'people are at their learning best while having fun.' When people have fun they open their minds and let go of their inhibitions... From my experience, people are at their learning best while participating in a sports ministry.' With an opportunity to have unobstructed time of sport and fun we are at our very best to learn what God has for us. Jesus loved using camping ministry. He took His disciples away from the hustle and bustle of the crowds. Jesus went on retreat to focus, talk to His Father and listen to Him. Throughout the Scriptures we see biblical heroes leaving for the wilderness to gain perspective. Moses and the children of Israel must have had the longest camping experience ever. The people were infected with pagan ideas and practices that God wanted to purge through their time in the desert.

What can we learn about a temporary system?

A temporary system:

- Helps take you away from the distractions and pressures of normal life.
- Gives you 100 per cent time with people.
- It creates a channel of 'shared experiences'.
- Is a fertile training ground. New places heighten your sense of awareness and help you concentrate.
- Creates an openness and vulnerability that can be hidden in daily routines.
- Can create a close loving community when it is centred on Christ. A camp setting, when focused on Christ, is a mountain-top experience. A taster of things to come, or things you may miss.
- Also helps you learn to develop Christian sportsmanship, living and playing together.
- It is also a fertile training ground for your young leaders. I am often more excited about my leaders than my athletes because it is giving them an experience of ministry they will build on for the rest of their lives.
- A sports camp creates an environment for holistic growth; it engages the whole person: mental, physical, social and spiritual.

Warnings:

- A Christian sports camp-retreat can open up serious turmoil in the heart of a camper that has been repressed. Spiritual battle takes place when someone allows God to break the chains of sin. It is a form of 'good grief'. Being sensitive to the movement of God in restoring a person is important. Some issues may be raised that you do not have the skill or training to address. Be prepared to bring in someone who can.
- The problem with the mountain top is you have to eventually go down. Let me again stress that an event big or small though significant is not complete ministry. The active strategy of rooting them into the life of a healthy church is the hard work.

SPORTS OUTREACH

Summer Sports Camp
Leaders Guide

*Much of this has been taken and adapted through the years from Sports Plus Summer Camps & Fellowship of Christian Athletes Sports Camps.

A letter from Steve Connor:

'And so, since God in His mercy has given us this wonderful ministry, we never give up!' (2 Cor. 4:1).

Welcome to Sports Camp!
It is great to have you on the team!

You are an integral part of our camp staff and I am thankful for your willingness and sacrifice to give up your time to be with us. Our theme this year is **'Run the Race'** and I could not think of a better group of leaders to 'run with'. I want to challenge you to stretch and raise your level! Whether you are a seasoned camp leader or just starting in ministry, push yourself to have the best week of your life, mentally, physically, socially and spiritually. If you were asked to play this week for your favourite team, how would you prepare? There is no coincidence you are going to Sports Outreach Scotland Camp, prepare for it as if God has invited you to lead His team.

It is our Christian service to glorify God in all that we are and do. God invites us to work alongside Him, and we are privileged to be part of His team. This will be a fantastic week to use what we love: Jesus, young athletes, sport... for ministry. That is what we are about: 'to glorify God in the world of sport'. **Please read through this booklet**. It may not all make sense until we go through the pre-camp training (**July 13, 11:00 sharp Queen Victoria School**) but be preparing ahead of time.

PRAY HARD - LIFE IS SHORT!

Camp Glossary:
Learn these words:

Dean - is the disciplinarian, hatchet man!

Huddle - old American football term for group. Sports Outreach Scotland Camp is organised in small groups that eat, and sleep together, but they may not all be interested in the same sport.

Huddle Leader - is a dorm or small group leader.

Coach - is a sports teacher, instructor.

Athletes - campers.

Team Meetings - an assembly of all the athletes, coaches and huddle leaders.

Huddle Banner - a wooden pole with your huddle number on it that you can decorate.

Huddle Banter - small group cheer.

Power Time - a time for entire camp to start their day!

THE PROGRAMME

SUNDAY

4:00	Welcome, Registration, Bank
5:30	Team Photo (In Camp Shirts)
6:00	Dinner
7:00	Huddle Meeting
7:15	Warm-up & Team Challenge
8:15	Evening Team Meeting
9:45	Huddle Meeting
11:00	Lights Out

MONDAY - THURSDAY

7:30	On the Green with the Dean (Optional)
7:45	Power Time: *warm-up, minute-message, focus-time*
8:00	Breakfast
9:00	Morning Team Meeting
9:45	Morning Training Session
11:00	(Huddle Leaders Meeting)
12:00	Lunch
12:30	(Coaches Meeting)
1:30	Afternoon Training Session (2nd Sport)
3:30	Option Time
5:00	Free Time
6:00	Dinner
7:00	Team Challenge

SPORTS OUTREACH

8:30	Evening Team Meeting
10:00	Huddle Meeting (Buzz Groups Tuesday & Wednesday)
11:00	Lights Out

FRIDAY

7:30	On the Green with the Dean (Optional)
7:45	Power Time: *warm-up, minute-message, focus-time*
8:00	Breakfast
9:00	Morning Team Meeting
9:45	Morning Training Session
10:45	Final Competition and leaders Challenge
12:00	Lunch & Pack
1:30	Team Meeting and Awards (*All bags taken to meeting*)
2:30	Depart

HUDDLE LEADERS' RESPONSIBILITIES

As a Huddle Leader you are responsible for a small group of young athletes (of the same sex). Your role is pastoral, encouraging them in their sport and understanding of Christ. You will work alongside another Huddle leader or be assisted by a coach depending on numbers. Below are some notes we will go through during 'Leaders Pre-camp Training', but I strongly encourage you to read through the whole booklet in advance.

Huddle Leaders' role includes:
- Participating in all pre-camp training.
- Assisting during registration.
- Monitoring Huddle needs.
- Keeping Huddle on schedule.
- Being on time!!!
- Eating together at meals.
- Loving and encouraging each other.
- Referring individuals with counselling needs to appropriate staff person (note: in case of child abuse you are legally obliged to refer individual; you do not have confidentiality status).
- Being enthusiastic.
- Being available to listen to campers when needed.
- Leading group and individual discipline.
- Being on time!!!
- Enforcing lights out and handling morning wake-up.
- Loving and encouraging each other.
- Not leaving huddles after lights out.

Huddle meetings:

- Be on time!!!
- Ensure huddle members know each other's names (name association).
- Guide discussion, involve entire huddle.
- Huddles eat most meals together and sit together at morning and evening team meetings.
- Guide and facilitate prayer.
- Plan and present evening devotions.
- Coaching sessions and team challenge.
- Actively assist in coaching sessions when time allows.
- Encourage and motivate athletes during coaching time.
- Encourage both teams during competition.
- Coach your huddle during Team Challenge, (women may play - needs to be discussed with the director).
- Encourage both teams during competition.
- Pray (encourage campers to lead prayer) after each competition.
- Encourage campers to get active in a church.

Post- camp responsibilities for Huddle Leaders

- Help in clean-up after sports camp.
- Maintain contact with each huddle member several times for at least one year.
- Write a letter to each athlete within first week to encourage him or her (this is a lifeline you are sending), and a Christmas card.
- Add campers on daily prayer list for a year. Have athletes sign your Bible.

COACH'S RESPONSIBILITIES

- Be prepared to coach your sport with excellence. Each coach will have a 'Head-Coach' who, depending on numbers, will be assisted by a assistant coaches. You will be required to give top-quality coaching from a Christian perspective. You are responsible to bring all equipment you will need to coach for the week.
- You are required to participate in all pre-camp training.
- You will have two (first and second) Sports specialities (up to four hours a day)
- Below are some notes we will go through during 'Leaders Pre-camp Training', but I strongly encourage you to read through the whole booklet in advance.

Coach's Role includes:

- You will assist with Team Challenge.
- Give Christian input during each coaching session.
- Assist during registration.
- Lead by example.
- Monitor Huddle needs (mainly for Huddle Leaders).
- Keep sports camp on time.

- Participate in all meetings.
- Love and encourage each other.
- Refer individuals with counselling needs to appropriate staff person (note: in case of child abuse you are legally obliged to refer individual; you do not have confidentiality status).
- Be enthusiastic.
- Instruct positively.
- Be available to athletes.
- Lead group and individual discipline.
- Lead 'on time'!!!
- Enforce lights out and handle morning wake-up.
- Love and encourage each other.
- Patrol lights out.
- Learn your athlete's names!
- Lead 'Power Break' water and (minute message).
- Attend all team meetings and coach's huddle meetings.
- Help enforce discipline during camp, especially during free time and Huddle leader meetings.
- Prepare an individual coaching critique and training plan for upcoming year.
- Encourage athletes to get active in a church.
- Referee and help organise Team Challenge.
- Share your testimony or minute message during each coaching session (Power Break).
- Introduce drills and training that will develop the individual athlete.
- Coach positively and build players up during week.
- Maintain a balance between being a disciplinarian and friend.
- Motivate athletes during week.
- Encourage Christian ethos during Team Challenge WWJD (women may play - needs to be discussed with the director).
- Pray (encourage campers to lead prayer) after each competition.
- Pray after each coaching session.
- Write individual evaluations for all athletes in your sport. (first sport only).

Post-camp responsibilities for coaches
- Help clean up camp
- Add campers on daily prayer list for a year. Have athletes sign your Bible.

OTHER NOTES:
We will cover these on - pre-camp training weekend
- Our goal for every individual at camp is to grow closer to Christ.
- First impressions are key.

- Athletes are the most important people at camp.
- Lights out: so they can enjoy camp.
- Rules are there to protect like a fence on a cliff, not to be rules for the sake of having rules.
- Do not gravitate towards other leaders.
- Everything is there to build up campers not tear down. Be careful of negative humour, would Jesus say it?
- Do not go off on tangents during meetings.
- Keep it simple, stay close to the cross. Satan loves to put up smoke screens. *'What about euthanasia'.*
- Always have Bible and name tag.
- Put name in Bible.
- Know everybody's name in Huddle!!!

In Huddle Meetings:

- Keep meetings moving like hot potatoes, not another preach session.
- Silence is okay.
- Encourage questions.
- Do not preach.
- Use Jesus' example of pointed questions.
- Four types of questions to ask and develop through your huddle meetings:
- Icebreaker questions: What is your favourite TV show? Why?
- Introductory questions: 'Did you learn any thing from the speaker?....'
- Defining questions: Why is that important?
- Application questions: (information without application is stagnation) How does this apply to you? (Many people are twelve inches away from being a Christian, they know it in their head, but they have not sown it in their hearts or applied it to their lives).

SPORTS OUTREACH

Teaching, Testimony, Talks... Christian Input

You will see from the programme that there is a Huddle Meeting each day, except Friday. If you are a Huddle leader it is your responsibility to plan and lead this small group bible study/discussion.

The Huddle Meeting provides an opportunity for team leader and the athletes in their team to discuss, pray and look at the Bible, following the theme of the main morning and evening meetings.

Leading the Huddle Meeting

Huddle leaders will be supplied with some discussion questions for use in the Huddle Meetings. These questions are simply a guide to help you start discussions and do not need to be followed rigidly. Keep the discussions focused on the subject or Bible text being discussed.

Looking at the Bible:

Here are three questions you could consider to help you as you prepare any Bible study:
- What does it say?
- What does it say about God?
- What does that mean for me?
- How do I respond?

We will spend some time during the training weekend looking at the team meetings and how to prepare and lead them. The following is simply some helpful information for you to consider in the meantime.

Use the team meetings as an opportunity to find out where the young people in your group are at spiritually - but be sensitive! You are likely to have a mixed group in which some people will never have heard the gospel and others will be committed Christians - this is both a challenge and an excellent opportunity for the young people to learn from you and each other.

You may want to start each team meeting with a short prayer and encourage the young people to be involved as the week progresses.

Tips for leading a Huddle
- Start and finish with a prayer. Encourage the young people to pray silently or aloud if they want to.
- Think of an interesting icebreaker, story or topic of conversation to open with - about their day/the talk/sport etc.
- Have the Bible open and encourage the group to read it aloud and/or in turn.

- Present the question in different ways, rephrase where necessary and make them relevant/topical, maybe with a sporting example or twist.
- Let the group give their own responses to the question, don't talk too much or always be giving them the answer. Keep it Bible-based and Christ-centred.
- Keep it short and sweet - don't be boring! If you don't enjoy it, the group probably won't.
- Be honest and don't compromise on the truth.
- Don't make it too formal, you are their friend as much as their teacher!
- Don't disappear at the end. Chat about other things, they may want to ask questions.
- Make sure you have prepared beforehand by looking at the passage, thinking of questions and praying.
- Tell them your story.

'Many of *the Samaritans from that town believed in Jesus because of the woman's testimony...*' (John 4:39).

We can see from the example of the Samaritan woman in John's Gospel how effective testimony can be. Whether you are a coach or a Huddle Leader you will probably have an opportunity to speak personally about your faith and how you became a Christian.

'*Always be* prepared *to give an answer to* everyone *who asks you to give* the reason *for* the hope *that you have. But do this with gentleness* and respect' (I Pet. 3:15).

How prepared are you?

Team building relationships

As a Huddle Leader or Coach, you will be one of the first leaders to meet the young people in your team (and possibly their parents!) at the welcome and registration. First impressions are important, so be friendly, fun and positive.

'*Do not imitate what is evil but what is* good' (3 John 11).

Be Imitators of Christ

When all of your team have been registered and received their welcome packs you will take them to your dorm-rooms, help them settle in and get them to dinner on time ready for Team Challenge. Eat with your Huddle.

Following dinner you go immediately to the first Team Challenge event - an inter-team competition in various sports running through the week. Build a positive atmosphere and good team spirit as quickly as possible.

Learn the names of each member of your Huddle quickly; they should be wearing name badges, so that helps!

Look out for individuals on the fringe of the team and try to pull the team together and involve everyone.

SPORTS OUTREACH

It is not your job to preach at the young people. You are not trying to have a deep philosophical conversation with every young person all of the time! You are trying to get alongside them in a genuine way and develop positive, encouraging, trusting relationships. We have to earn the right and respect to present them with challenging and thought-provoking questions. Get to know the young people: about their families, interests, sport, school life, etc. Be interested in them.

You must devote some quality time on a one-to-one basis to each member of your team at some time during camp - but don't corner them. Keep it relaxed and informal.

You must also do this safely and sensibly. If you are alone with a member of your group try to make sure other adults can see you and another adult knows where you are. This may mean chatting in a dorm with the door open, or on the field in clear view of others, or in the tuck shop or canteen area. Make sure you avoid quiet, isolated areas and if in doubt ask another leader to join you. Be careful with physical touch (**Refer to the 'Safe From Harm' document for further guidelines and ensure that you have read this fully).**

If there are Christians in your Huddle your aim is to disciple, encourage and strengthen them in their faith. When they leave camp you could agree with them on an aspect of their Christian faith they can work on. With the non-Christian young people in the Huddle your aim is to explain the gospel to them clearly and simply.

Both of these aims will be achieved through the combination of many aspects of camp; the Team meetings; Huddle meetings; and individual contact with leaders, coaches and general helpers.

Your role is an important and exciting one as you seek to proclaim the gospel clearly and faithfully to the young people and build up those maturing in their Christian commitment.

Care and Encouragement

IMPORTANT FOR ALL

Please ensure that you have read the 'Safe From Harm' policy document published by Sports Outreach Scotland. This will be provided during pre camp training.

Sports Outreach Scotland aims to encourage good practice amongst the leaders, coaches and general helpers running the camp to ensure that the young people attending may do so safely. It is therefore important that you read the 'Safe From Harm' document, which gives clear guidelines for the ways of working to ensure safe practice.

_____ is Chaplain and will act as 'Children's Advocate' for the week.

Your attitude towards the young people should always be positive - building the young people up rather than pulling them down. It takes many positive comments to make amends for one negative comment. Be consistent in your encouragement and don't show favouritism. *Jesus said, 'Let the little children come to me, and do not hinder them, for the kingdom of heaven belongs to such as these'* (Matt. 19:14).

The young people are important - Jesus said so. It is hard work loving and caring for your Huddle for a whole week, so get some good nights' sleep before you come to camp so that you are ready and fresh, and willing to give to the young people.

As your Huddle competes in the Team Challenge competition you will play a vital role in encouraging and motivating them. Develop a positive and fair competitive attitude. You are their coach during Team Challenge and should make sure that someone prays after each competition.

Each evening a Huddle will be nominated to win the 'Huddle of the Day' award. The award criteria include: team spirit, discipline, timekeeping, attendance, behaviour, encouragement, politeness, Team Challenge results and attitude. In fact, anything that is good and positive and seeks to build up the camp.

A little inter-team competition for winning the Team of the Day award is healthy, especially if the young people are motivated to be positive and encouraging, but be cautious not to develop too much rivalry or negative attitudes towards other teams.

Finally, if at any time you are concerned about any member of your Huddle, maybe they are: homesick, troublesome, ill, showing signs of abuse, whatever, the Chaplain is your first port of call for help. They are there to help and support you as you care for your team and if they are not able to help, they will direct you to someone who can.

We have a full team of workers with much pastoral and leadership experience. The team is put together for the benefit of us all -- young people and leaders alike.

Discipline and Organisation

By discipline we do not, under any circumstances, mean that you are permitted to hit or strike any young person at camp. If you lay down fair and workable ground rules and set your expectations for attitude and behaviour clearly at the start of camp, discipline should not be a problem.

Just as all games have rules so that we can maximise our enjoyment of them and be kept from harm, so camp also has rules for the very same reason. The following set of camp rules will be given to each young person and are given to you now to ensure continuity and consistency of their adherence throughout camp.

Camp Rules

It goes without saying that as a leader, coach or general helper, you are expected to set an example by following these rules also.

- Aim to make friends with everyone in your team.

- When speaking, always ensure it is to build people up and not pull down.

- Respect everyone. We are all valuable and precious.

- Respect other peoples' property and sports equipment.

- As part of the above, do not go into other peoples' dorms or go off school property without permission from the Dean or the Director.

SPORTS OUTREACH

- Be on time, set an example to others.

- Fully participate in the programme for maximum benefit and enjoyment.

- Any problems with illness or injury, please see physio and keep Huddle leader informed.

- All medicines are to be handed in to the physio and dispensed at meal times.

- If you are sick, do not leave or ring home to leave without permission from the Director or the Huddle leader co-ordinator.

- No smoking, no alcohol, no non-prescription drugs, no fires, no electrical gadgets of any kind. If brought with you, please hand in for safe keeping.

- No one is to go off school property without permission of programme director, Dean or Director (including Huddle Leaders).

- The schedule is not optional.

- Illness should be reported to Huddle leader.

- No biting of ears.

- No bad language.

- Anything else the Dean may think of!

The Dean, _____ and his 'able assistant' _____, are the face of discipline, control and authority on the camp, in both a serious and a fun way. Any camp discipline problems will be addressed by the Dean. Additionally, if you do have any discipline problems with individuals in your team, please consult the Dean, _____; Programme Director, _____; the Chaplain _____ or the Camp Director, in that order.

If camp is to run effectively it is important that the young people know exactly when and where they are doing things. It is a good idea for Huddle leaders and coaches to run through the programme with their athletes - they will each get a copy.

Huddle leaders will need to work hard on the following areas with their Huddle if they are to be organised and stand any chance of getting the Huddle of the Day award!

Time Keeping - you MUST BE ON TIME! Being late for any session may mean you miss important notices and delay the day's programme - it can not happen! Run to different events.

Attendance - All sessions should be fully attended by all of your Huddle. The only time that young people are not expected in one particular place is during free time at 16h45.

Togetherness - Unity within your Huddle is important, no-one should be left out.

Equipment - Make sure the athletes take all they need in their bags in the morning. We do not want individuals wandering back to the dorms unattended. If it is essential, make sure they are accompanied by another person, preferably a leader.

Name Badges - These should be worn at all times, except during physical activity. It is a good idea for you to collect and distribute them for the whole group - they get lost easily!

Water Bottles - The athletes are exected to have water bottles, encourage them to use them. They are doing a lot of physical activity and need to keep taking on water throughout the whole day. Have a '**Team Drink**' after each competition.

Sun Cream - Assuming we have good weather (?!) remind the young people to use sun cream when necessary and wear caps in intense sun/heat.

Leading by Example

One of sport's unique qualities is that it quickly creates an atmosphere for building relationships. God's love will be proclaimed both **formally** (through the main talks and team meetings) and **informally** (building relationships).

Our heartfelt prayer for you is that you are enthusiastic about Jesus, Camp, sport and your particular role as a Huddle Leader or Coach. It is this enthusiasm which will rub off on the young people we are there to serve. In fact, more than anything else, our enthusiastic attitude will be our greatest unspoken witness. As we have mentioned, many of the young people will not have any sort of Christian background and they will be making their judgements about Christ based on what they see in us.

'We are therefore Christ's Ambassadors, as though God were making his appeal through us. We implore you on Christ's behalf. Be reconciled to God' (2 Cor. 5:20).

We are Therefore Christ's Ambassadors

What a **privilege** to be considered worthy enough to be an Ambassador for Christ, even in our weakness and sin, to be representing Him to others. God is gracious.

What a **responsibility** we have as an ambassador to be faithful in how we represent Christ, in both our words and actions, to remain faithful to the truth of the gospel.

What an **opportunity** we have as an ambassador of Christ to serve others with the same attitude of love and service as He did, to present Christ and the gospel to young people who have not heard it.

SPORTS OUTREACH

May we **support and encourage** each other to wholeheartedly accept the privilege, responsibility and opportunity to be Christ's ambassadors to the young people on camp.

Huddle Leaders should remember that you are **not** primarily coaches during the sport training sessions, you **are** Huddle leaders first and foremost. You can help out with coaching when time permits, by all means join in (with permission of the coach) - this will develop your team building with some of your group, but be sensible with your time. We will be having a compulsory Huddle leader Bible study during the second half of Morning Training Session (11:00 - 12:00) each day. Coaches' Bible studies will take place after lunch (12:30).

Where possible there will be two Huddle leaders to each Huddle; some Huddles will have a coach linked with them. It is important therefore, that you work well together, work out each other's strengths and weaknesses, and support and encourage each other in both. We will talk more about the different helper roles, in addition to the programme details during our sessions at the training weekend.

It is essential that we are familiar with the schools, the venues for the sports and meetings, the programme and the routines of camp. It is also important for us to spend time together as a leadership team, to develop a strong, supportive team spirit before the young people arrive on the Sunday. We will also have a chance to play a bit of sport too!

Don't worry if you do not understand everything now - that's why we have a training weekend! We will also have our daily meetings during camp to address issues as they arise, pray together and support each other. Have a read through this booklet again and see if there are any areas in which you can make some preparations - maybe read a book. Please make sure you go through the checklist on the back page. If you have any questions at all, please don't hesitate to contact:

Finally, a few words of encouragement:

Jesus says to Paul:
'My grace is sufficient for you, for my power Is made perfect In weakness'
(2 Cor. 12:9).

'Do not be ashamed to testify about our Lord'
(1 Tim. 1:7-8).

'The one who calls you Is faithful and he will do It'
(I Thess. 5:24).

SPORTS OUTREACH

 Appendix 6

Sports Outreach Golf Outing
_____ Golf Club

Dear _____

Our church Sports Outreach team would like to welcome you to the annual Church outing at _____Golf Club. This is a day where we will see the competitive spirit, those needing holes in their pockets stitched up and those who should stick to fishing or doing the dishes!!

Nevertheless, we will have a great time together culminating at a dinner and presentation at the _____, in the evening where _____ will speak about their Christian faith in the sports world.

OUTLINE for the day:

Total Golf Cost: _____ (includes green fees, coffee & bacon roll on arrival, and a contribution to the prizes).

Meal cost: _____ plus tip (3 courses, menu enclosed)

Drinks: These should be paid for individually on the evening.

Timings: Leave 9am sharp from _____(abandon cars!!)
            Coffee & Bacon Rolls 10.00am
            Rules of the day 11.00am
            First tee off time 11.20am

Evening Meal: Meet at the _____ with a partner if appropriate for drinks 7pm. The meal will begin at 7.30pm.

Prizes: 9pm approx.

We have all looked forward to this day so do your best to enjoy yourselves, introduce yourself to new people and all in all make it another day to remember.

Sports Outreach Golf Groupings

Martin Macsmith 7	Mac Macsmith 20	Simon MacSmith 18	Carl MacSmith 16
Russell Smith 5	Clark Smith 15	Nick Smith 16	Angus MacSmith 18
Sandy Macsmith 7	Alister MacSmith 20	Lesley MacSmith 10	Big Al MacSmith 18
Steve MacSmith 20	Scott MacSmith 18	Phil MacSmith 18	Barry MacSmith 18
Ollie Smith 20	Douglas Smith 20	Donald Smith 20	David Smith 20
Stuart Smith 9	David Smith 14	Mark Smith 20	Davie Smith 18
John Smith 20	John Smith 18	Hugh Smith 15	

(non- regular players have been allocated an additional 2 strokes)

- Each group should tee off at 8-minute intervals and seek to keep play moving at all times. In the interest of fast play, putts within a distance of 6' may be given unless the playing partners feel that due to the degree of difficulty, or debate with distance, it must be putted. Players should *not* assume that the putt is automatically given!!

- Should a group find itself looking for balls and identify that those behind are sleeping, the moon is coming out or other playing partners are reading a book, it is in order to pick up your ball and move to the next tee. It can get better!! It is a stableford therefore if you are out of the points, then in order to keep play moving could you please pick up.

- The rules of golf should be applied throughout the round and where there is a question on a situation or a ruling needed the playing partners should be asked; if in further doubt, it should be raised at the end with the committee to determine the right decision.

- Balls should NOT be moved, touched or interfered with during the round. In the sand, the club should not be grounded!! Please do not let the competitive spirit get the better off of you!! There will be random drug tests; pockets searched for duplicate balls and members of the SAS in the bushes watching the play on the day.

- Please ensure you know what ball you are playing with and either mark it or ensure that it is not duplicated in type and number by other playing partners. To play the wrong ball constitutes penalty strokes!! Players should declare to other playing partners the ball they have chosen to play with.

- When marking your ball on the green it must be replaced exactly where you picked it up. Any attempts to gather inches will necessitate some serious eye testing as well as a penalty stroke.

- You should declare to your playing partners the exact number and make of ball you are playing with. If during the round you need to change or replace the ball, again you should inform your playing partners.

- As for arithmetic!!! Please display your 'O' level at the first tee remembering that to get it wrong renders your score as 'nil'. A playing partner should mark your card and should sign on completion of the round. Every shot is counted!!

- Highest individual stableford for the day (3 points for Birdie, 2 for Par and 1 for Bogie).

- Match play: best ball in the foursomes (2v2)

- Group stableford: cumulative points from your fourball.

- Nearest the pin @ hole 4 and 17.

- Longest Drive @ hole 18.

- 'Worst round of his life'- - - 'Best Tryer'

- Best at par 3's, gross score.

- Best net score (gross score minus handicap on the day)

- Best gross score on the day

- Best dressed golfer

- Most gross birdies on the day

- Players should mark their gross score on the cards and have them duly checked and signed at the end of the round. Failure to do this will result in you not getting your dinner and being sent to your bed. Scorecards should not be completed by yourself and should be given to a team member at the beginning of the round.

- The longest drive must clearly be on the fairway and should you find yourself on the road on the M9, this will not count!! (No lawnmowers in bag please!!)

- Where the score at a hole is looking more like your overdraft or you find yourself wishing you had a calculator, could you please, in the interest of sanity, please pick up!!

From the church Sports Outreach committee we welcome you today and hope that you have a great sporting time and enjoy the company of your fellow golfers.

HAVE A GREAT DAY!!!

* Thanks to the Stirling XY Team for putting this together.

Appendix 7

Introduction to 'Sports Outreach Teams' (Small Groups)

The 'Sports Outreach' meeting is the heart of the whole ministry concept. A 'Sports Outreach Team' is like a 'huddle', an American football term for when the team gathers together on the pitch and implements various plays and strategy. A sports ministry 'Huddle' (small group) is for inquirers and Christians seeking to learn, discuss and implement the sporty life within a Christian context. Research suggests that most people from unchurched backgrounds attribute their conversion to Christianity by the influence of a Christian friend - relationships. Sport provides an excellent way of making friends and building relationships, these can be developed into evangelistic opportunities.

Small group meetings link the 'Big Events' and Camps into a series of consistent opportunities for proclaiming God's Word and encouraging spiritual growth. Many of us have been to outreach functions where we have seen youth and adults indicate that they have trusted Christ as Lord and Saviour. What an exciting time to see those for whom we have been praying apparently open up their hearts to Christ.

However, joy can turn to disappointment as we realize that not all the youth that have made a profession of faith are growing in their relationship to Christ. Why do some seem to wilt on the vine? Possibly many causes, but all too often the problem is a lack of carry-on or follow-up from more mature Christians.

The church is seeing the value in having a ministry to the sports world. 'It's a knock-out', five-a-side's, and pool parties have been part of the arsenal of every youth group for years. But what comes next? Often a young person whose whole life revolves around sport will be discontent with the youth group or club geared to music or drama. Sports Outreach Teams focus on presenting Christ's salvation and His Lordship in a way that interests sporty young people.

The how's, when's, where's and who's

How often should we meet?
The answer to this question varies. Some group leaders will want to meet every week while others will meet once or twice a term. Whatever you do, plan the meetings well and be consistent. Weekly meetings have historically been most effective.

When do Sports Outreach Teams meet?
Again the answer is varied. Whether you meet after church, during club time, lunch, evenings, after school, before training or after training, early mornings before work, or Saturdays after a round of golf. Survey your group and choose the best possible time.

Where should we meet?

Many Christian groups are successful because they meet at their local church or school property in a central location. Still others like having a place that is away from church or school, the atmosphere can be less formal or classroomy. Each group will have to survey their area to see which kind of setting will best accomplish their goals - to lead sports people to Christ and help them to mature in their faith. Our best model of small groups in the United Kingdom has been the Alpha Course. Many of their meetings are at night and centred around a meal.

Who leads the team?

Sports Outreach leaders need three criteria: to love Jesus, to love people and to love sport, and in that order! Obviously by now if you have read this far into the book you are interested in developing a sports ministry. From experience we want to encourage you to get help and prayer support. Leaders should take care not to dominate the meetings but rather, to facilitate discussion.

In the book of Titus we find the young man Titus was left on the island of Crete to organize the Cretan Christians into churches. Over and over Paul tells Titus to encourage the Cretans to 'do what is good'.

'Similarly, encourage the young men to be self-controlled. In everything set them a good example by doing what is good. In your teaching show integrity, seriousness and soundness of speech that cannot be condemned, so that those who oppose you may be ashamed because they have nothing bad to say about us' (Titus 2:6-8).

Sports Outreach Teams:

Discovery Team (ISBN 1-85792-870-9)

Impact Team (ISBN 1-85792-871-7)

Leadership Team (ISBN 1-85792-872-5)

These Bible Study Guides are available at Christian Bookstores and from Christian Focus Publications - www.christianfocus.com

Appendix 8

Podium Illustration

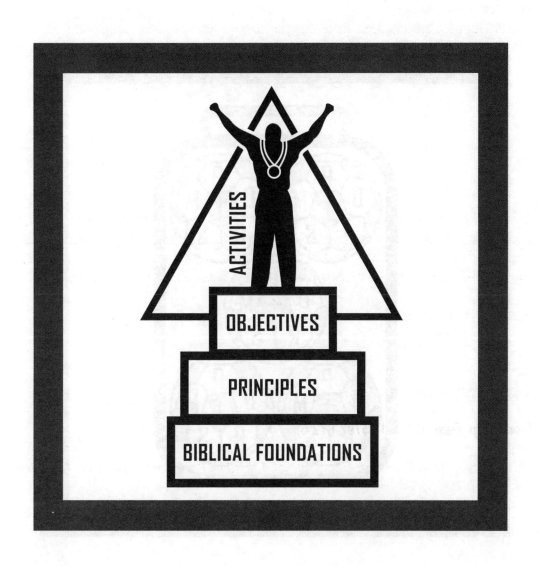

SPORTS OUTREACH

 Appendix 9

Jar Illustration

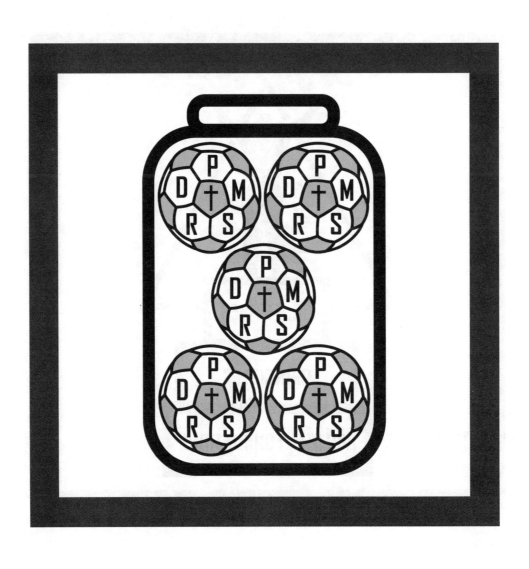

Index

Bibliography

Aldrich, Joseph C *Life Style Evangelism* (Multnomah Press, 1978).

Allen, Roland *Missionary Methods*(Wm. B Eerdmans Publishing Company, 1962).

Bruce, A B *The Training of the Twelve,* (Kregel Publications, 1971).

Coleman, Robert E *The Master Plan of Evangelism,* (Fleming H Revell, Baker Book House Company, 1963).

Connor, Steve *A Sporting Guide to Eternity* (Christian Focus Publications, Tain, 2002).

Covey, Stephen R *The 7 Habits of Highly Effective People* (Fireside,Simon & Schuster, 1989).

Green, Michael *Evangelism Through the Local Church* (Hodder & Stoughton,1990).

Handley, Rod *Character Counts, Who's Counting Yours?* (Cross Training Publishing, 1995).

Hughes, R Kent *Living on the Cutting Edge* (Crossway Books, 1987).

Kendall, R T *Understanding Theology, The Means of Developing a Healthy Church in the 21st Century* (Christian Focus Publications, Tain, 1996)

Ladd,Tony & James Mathisen *Muscular Christianity: Evangelical Protestants and the Development of American Sports* (Baker Books, 1999).

Little, Paul *How to give away your Faith,* (Intervarsity Press, 1966).

MacPerry, John *The Bible: Why Trust It?* (Haven Books, 1980).

McDowell, Josh *Evidence that Demands a Verdict,* (Here's Life Publishers, Inc. 1972).

McGrath, Alister *Bridge Building, Communicating Christianity effectively* (Inter-Varsity Press 1993).

Packer, J I *Concise Theology, a Guide to Christian Historic Beliefs* (Tyndale, 1993).

Senter III, Mark H *Four Views of Youth Ministry and the Church,* (Zondervan Publishing, 2001).

Stewart, Tracey *Payne Stewart* (Broadman & Holman, 2000).

Strommen, Merton; Karen E Jones, Dave Rahn *Youth Ministry That Transforms* (Zondervan)

Thomas, Bob & Greg Lewis *Good Sports* (Zondervan Publishing House, 1994).

Timmis, Stephen *Multiplying Churches, Reading Today's Communities Through Church Planting,* (Christian Focus Publishing, 2000).

Warren, Rick *The Purpose Driven Church* (Zondervan Publishing, 1995).

Weir, Stuart *What the Book Says About Sport* (Bible Reading Fellowship, 2000).

Weir, Stuart *More than Champions* (Marshall Pickering, 1993).

Christian Focus Publications publishes books for all ages

Our mission statement -

STAYING FAITHFUL

In dependence upon God we seek to help make His infallible word, the Bible, relevant. Our aim is to ensure that the Lord Jesus Christ is presented as the only hope to obtain forgiveness of sin, live a useful life and look forward to heaven with Him.

REACHING OUT

Christ's last command requires us to reach out to our world with his gospel. We seek to help fulfill that by publishing books that point people towards Jesus and for them to develop a Christ-like maturity. We aim to equip all levels of readers for life, work, ministry and mission.

Books in our adult range are published in three imprints.

Christian Heritage contains classic writings from the past.
Mentor focuses on books written at a level suitable for Bible College and seminary students, pastors, and other serious readers; the imprint includes commentaries, doctrinal studies, examination of current issues and church history.
Christian Focus contains popular works including biographies, commentaries, basic doctrine and Christian living. Our children's books are also published in this imprint.

For a free catalogue of all our titles, please write to:
Christian Focus Publications, Ltd
Geanies House, Fearn,
Ross-shire, IV20 1TW, Scotland,
United Kingdom
info@christianfocus.com

For details of our titles visit us on our website
www.christianfocus.com